AUSTRALIA'S
Wet Tropics
Rainforest Life

including the Daintree Region

Clifford & Dawn Frith

Mt. Bellenden Ker

Published in Australia
by **FRITH & FRITH** Books
'Prionodura', P. O. Box 581,
Malanda, Queensland 4885
Telephone (070) 96 0105
Facsimile (070) 96 8316

National Library of Australia
Card Number ISBN 0 9589942 7 7

First printed 1992

Other books in this series:

Australian Tropical Birds
Australian Tropical Reptiles and Frogs
Australian Tropical Reef Life
Australian Tropical Butterflies
Australian Tropical Orchids
Australia's Cape York Peninsula

Leaves of Bumpy Ash tree

Preface

The rainforests of the Australian Wet Tropics cover an area of seven thousand five hundred square kilometres and occur between Cooktown and Townsville (see map, page 71). This is considerably less than existed prior to European settlement. South of the Daintree River extensive areas of lowland rainforest were cleared for sugar cane farms. On the Atherton Tableland large areas were cleared for cattle grazing, or were clear-felled for timber, leaving small fragmented pockets of rainforest such as remain today around the crater lakes of Mount Hypipamee, Lake Eacham and Lake Barrine. Whilst much of the remaining rainforest has been heavily logged, some areas of unlogged rainforest remain, particularly on steeper slopes and in less accessible areas. One of the largest stands of relatively unspoilt rainforest in the Wet Tropics extends from the Bloomfield River to just north of Mount Carbine and includes spectacular lowland rainforests from Cape Tribulation to the Daintree River (see map, page 71). This is one of the few areas on earth where pristine tropical rainforest can be seen to all but meet a fringing coral reef.

In October 1980 the Australian Heritage Commission recognised the priceless value of Australia's remaining tropical rainforest and listed many areas on the Register of the National Estate. In 1984 the Commission requested that the Rainforest Conservation Society of Queensland prepare a report on the conservaton significance of North Queensland's tropical rainforests. During the early eighties there was immense public concern about the continuing destruction of Australia's tropical rainforests, particularly the logging of diverse virgin rainforest at Downey Creek and on Mount Windsor Tableland, and the construction of the infamous Cape Tribulation to Bloomfield Road (see map, page 71). It was during this period that we published two little books about our tropical rainforests, titled 'Australian Tropical Rainforest Life' and 'A Walk in the Rainforest'.

It was not until December 1988 that the rainforests of the Wet Tropics were officially placed on the World Heritage List, having fulfilled all the criteria required for inclusion as a natural heritage of outstanding global significance. In March 1990 an historic agreement was reached between the Prime Minister of Australia and Premier of Queensland for the joint management of the Wet Tropics of Queensland World Heritage Area and, as a result of this, the Wet Tropics Management Authority has been established with an agency based in Cairns. About eighty five percent of the tropical rainforest of the Wet Tropics is listed within the World Heritage Area. This includes not only the previously protected rainforest within the National Parks but also rainforest within State Forest, Timber Reserves and the Aboriginal and Islander Reserve at Yarrabah, south of Cairns.

At the time of European contact the region between Cooktown and Ingham was the traditional home of some twelve Aboriginal societies that primarily utilised rainforest for their livelihood. Indeed, the association between Aboriginal People and tropical rainforests dates back a long time. An archaeological site in a rock shelter in the Russell River Valley has yielded remains that are some 5100 years old. These rainforests were certainly rich in resources useful to the rainforest-dwelling Aborigines – plant materials for making woven baskets, long wooden 'swords' and shields, bark blankets and huts; plant chemicals for fish poisons and medicines and, most importantly, plant foods. Innumerable stone artifacts, such as axes, grindstones, hammerstones and nutcracking stones have been found in areas once covered by rainforest but now cleared.

Our tropical rainforests are of immense scientific value. They have provided refuges for many species that are regarded as relicts of an ancient fauna and flora that dates back as far as the breaking up of Gondwanaland (see page 2). The highest diversity of animal and plant life anywhere in Australia occurs within the wet tropical rainforests, with many species endemic, or peculiar, to the area. They also contain a reservoir of potentially useful pharmaceuticals and chemical compounds.

The Wet Tropics is a wilderness area of exceptional natural beauty with sweeping tropical sandy beaches, spectacular mountain ranges, deep gorges and picturesque waterfalls. The recreational value of the Wet Tropics is quickly becoming a major feature of the growing tourist industry. More and more visitors come to this area each year to enjoy two of the richest and most diverse ecosystems on earth – tropical reefs and rainforests. Rainforest interpretive centres have recently been established, particularly in the Daintree area, to provide an introductory guide to the rainforest ecosystem. National Parks, such as those at Mount Spec, Lake Barrine, Lake Eacham and Mossman Gorge (see map, page 71), have walking tracks that enable visitors to stroll through and enjoy the beauty of these magnificant wilderness areas. For information concerning readily accessible tropical rainforest locations, and the facilities each has to offer, visitors should contact the Queensland National Parks and Wildlife Service offices in Cairns, Cardwell, Townsville or Brisbane.

In the first part of this book we simply explain the fundamental ecology of rainforest life, how the rainforest is structured and how plants and animals closely inter-relate on the forest floor and within the understorey and canopy. The second part of the book deals with some of the animals that can be seen within this tropical habitat. We hope this illustrated introductory account will provide a greater understanding of the complexity of life in this most intricate, but fragile, of earth's ecosytems.

Clifford and Dawn Frith,
Tropical North Queensland

Introduction

Tropical rainforest is the richest of all earth's environments, where diverse plant and animal life co-exist in an intricately complex ecosystem. The whole tropical rainforest, from tree roots to the top of its canopy, is a living and dynamic entity. Tropical rainforests of the world cover some thirteen million square kilometres of the earth, in South America, Africa, Indo-Malaysia, Indonesia, New Guinea and Australia.

In Australia rainforests occur predominantly along the east coast, in a broken chain from Cape York south to Tasmania, and cover only about twenty thousand square kilometres, or a mere quarter of a percent, of the land surface. From north to south there are three main climatic types of rainforest: tropical, subtropical and temperate. Tropical rainforests are restricted to north-eastern Queensland and within this region they occur in two main biogeographical zones; those of Cape York Peninsula, and those of the Wet Tropics. The tropical rainforests of Cape York Peninsula occur predominantly near Bamaga, at the head of the Jardine River, Iron Range and McIlwraith Range. These forests receive less wet season rain than those of the Wet Tropics and are separated from them by a dry corridor from just south of the McIlwraith Range to Cooktown (see map, page 71).

Australia's largest area of tropical rainforests occurs between Cooktown and Townsville (see map, page 71). Because this area receives a higher rainfall than anywhere else in Australia it has become known as the Wet Tropics. Vegetation of the Wet Tropics is predominantly rainforest but also includes small patches of tall open forests and woodlands in the uplands, paperbark swamps in the lowlands and mangrove forests along the coast.

Evolutionary History

The flora and fauna of Australian tropical rainforests are of mixed origin and relate to the four major stages in the earth's evolutionary history. About one hundred and sixty million years ago Australia formed part of the vast southern continent known as Gondwanaland which also included New Zealand, South America, South Africa and Antarctica. This huge land mass started to fragment, and continents drifted slowly apart. Australia broke away from Antarctica some fifty million years ago and drifted northwards towards the equator carrying a unique fraction of the flora and fauna of Gondwanaland with it. Some fifty to one hundred million years ago wet forests were widespread and covered most of the Australian continent.

After its separation from Antarctica, Australia was an isolated land mass for about thirty five million years. During this second stage in its evolutionary history many new plants and animals evolved from the ancient Gondwanic life forms and diversified to form the more typical Australian flora and fauna. Global climates changed and Australia became more arid, and with this increasing aridity Australia's unique sclerophyll vegetation evolved and spread across the continent. Rainforests slowly contracted to wetter areas along the east coast.

About fifteen million years ago the composition of the flora and fauna underwent its third major change. The Australian Plate collided with the Asian Plate creating what we now call the Indonesian Archipelago, opening the way for an intermingling of species of two continental floras and faunas. The glacial periods that occurred during the last seventy thousand years (the last being about ten thousand years ago) brought about major fluctuations in the composition of the rainforest community. During this fourth stage sea levels changed and land bridges were exposed across the Torres Strait, between New Guinea and Cape York Peninsula, allowing an interchange between their floras and faunas.

What remains of our tropical rainforests today are but a relict of the type of vegetation that once covered the continent. The remaining patches of rainforest are referred to as refugial areas and within them many ancient plants and animals are still to be found. Thirteen of the world's nineteen primitive flowering plant, or angiosperm, families occur in the rainforests of the Wet Tropics. Two primitive plants, *Idiospermum australiense* and *Austrobaileya scandens*, are the world's only representatives of their respective families, the Idiospermaceae and the Austrobaileyaceae. The pollen of the *Austrobaileya* resembles one of the oldest known pollen types on earth. Some species of insects, frogs, reptiles, birds and marsupials are regarded as relicts of the ancient Gondwanan fauna. These include Peripatus (see page 22), the Chameleon and Leaf-tailed Geckos (see pages 30 & 31), the Southern Cassowary, the megapodes (see pages 38-40), the Musky Rat-kangaroo and the ringtail possums (see pages 61-66).

Flora and Fauna

Our wet tropical rainforests have the greatest species diversity of plants and animals in Australia. There are about twelve hundred species of flowering plants, or angiosperms, of which about one third are restricted to these rainforests. This number not only includes the rainforest trees, numbering more than eight hundred species, but also the orchids, gingers, cordylines, palms, pandanus and an immense variety of climbing plants. Besides flowering plants, there exist a bewildering variety of fungi, lichens, mosses, ferns, cycads and zamias.

The diversity of animals found in the wet tropical rainforests is great. Moths, butterflies, beetles, tree frogs, geckoes, forest dragons, tree monitors, pythons, cassowaries, pigeons, kingfishers, parrots, robins, honeyeaters, bowerbirds, bandicoots, brushtail and ringtail possums, tree-kangaroos and flying-foxes are just some of the animals that may be encountered in this habitat. Many of the species are peculiar, or endemic, to the rainforests of the Wet Tropics, whilst others also occur in the rainforests of Cape York Peninsula and/or those of New Guinea.

Mt. Lewis

Location

The rainforests of the Wet Tropics are located between latitudes 15°29' and 19°10' south and longitudes 144°52' and 146°31' east where they occupy a narrow belt along coastal plains, foothills, mountain ridges and tablelands from sea level to 1600 (average 600 to 900) metres above sea level. Rainforest also occurs on some offshore continental islands, such as Dunk and Hinchinbrook.

Much scenery of the Wet Tropics is quite stunning. The coast from Cedar Bay and the Bloomfield River southwards to Cape Tribulation (**opposite above**) and the Daintree River (**page i**) is most picturesque. Long sweeping white coral beaches, overhung with cottonwoods and stately huge laurels, and dense mangrove forests separate the rainforest from the fringing coral reef (**right**). It is one of the few wilderness areas in the world where two highly complex environments, still in their pristine state, meet – the rainforest and coral reef. The giant granitic outcrops on the summits of Mount Pieter Botte (928 metres above sea level) and Thornton Peak (1374 metres), the wide rainforested valley of Roaring Meg Creek, and the photogenic Daintree River are just a few natural features of immense beauty in this northern area of the Wet Tropics.

Further south are the spectacular deep gorges of the Mossman, Barron, Johnstone (**right below**), Russell, Mulgrave and Herbert Rivers, and numerous superb waterfalls including Tully, Blencoe and Wallaman Falls. The latter falls descends two hundred and seventy eight metres into a deep canyon to join the Herbert River and is one of the deepest single drops in Australia. The imposing ridges of the Bellenden Ker Range, with the highest peak of Mount Bartle Frere (1622 metres), dominate the landscape between Cairns and Innisfail (**opposite below**). The beautiful rainforested ancient crater lakes of Lake Barrine, Lake Eacham and Mount Hypipamee are unique features of the Atherton Tableland. The mountain backbone and the towering peak of Mount Bowen (1121 metres) form an impressive backdrop to the coastal rainforests around Hinchinbrook Island.

Climate

Tropical rainforests are subjected to two distinct climatic seasons – the 'wet' and 'dry'. Mean annual rainfall varies from twelve hundred to more than four thousand millimetres, with some areas receiving even higher falls; and over sixty percent of this rain falls during the wet season months. The wet season, from December to March, brings with it higher temperatures, torrential rain and very high humidity. The wettest areas are around Babinda and Tully and the adjacent Bellenden Ker Range (see map, page 71). Mount Bartle Frere is most often enveloped in cloud and receives some nine thousand millimetres of rain a year. Cyclones may also occur during the wet season months resulting in a major increase to seasonal rainfall. On the coast the average maximum temperatures in the wet summer are between 30-32°, and in the dry winter are between 13-20° centigrade, those of the tablelands are a few degrees lower. Frosts do occasionally occur on the tablelands.

Cape Tribulation

Palmerston National Park

Daintree to Bloomfield coast

Mt Bartle Frere, from the west

Mt. Bellenden Ker apex

Mt. Spec National Park, Paluma

Daintree River area

RAINFOREST STRUCTURE AND STRATA

More than eight hundred species of trees occur within the rainforests of the Wet Tropics. Rainforest trees include such well known species as the silky oaks, macadamias, waratahs and the Wheel of fire (family Proteaceae); the eugenias, lilly pillies, satinashes (family Myrtaceae); the jittas, silkwoods, euodias, aspens and bumpy ash (Rutaceae); the quandongs and carabeens (Elaeocarpaceae); the laurels and walnuts (Lauraceae); the cedars, rosewoods and mahoganies (Meliaceae); the legumes, such as the Black Bean (Fabaceae); the fig trees (Moraceae); and the umbrella trees (Araliaceae).

Not all rainforests of the Wet Tropics are floristically the same by any means, and thirteen different structural types have been recognised. This variation is related to such factors as rainfall, altitude, soil type and parent rock. Parent rock may be granitic, metamorphic (such as slate and schist), volcanic, basaltic, or alluvium. There are many different soil types; some may be of red or yellow loam, whilst others have a high sand or clay content.

Rainforests that grow in warmer wetter areas on rich soil are floristically more diverse and complex and their trees tend to have larger leaves. These rainforests, referred to as Mesophyll Vine Forests (**left**), occur mostly in lowland areas. They are the most luxuriant of all Australian rainforest types and are characterised by robust woody lianas, epiphytic ferns, palms such as the Fan Palm, *Licuala ramsayi* (**page 14**), strangler figs and gingers. Rainforests that grow in drier and colder areas on poorer soils tend to have smaller leaves. These rainforests, referred to as Notophyll Vine Forests, occur mostly in upland areas (**opposite below**). They also have robust woody lianas, strangler figs and epiphytic ferns; but tree ferns, climbing vines and mosses appear to be more abundant. Trees growing on exposed windswept ridges, such as on Mount Bartle Frere and Mount Bellenden Ker, are stunted and have even smaller leaves (**opposite above**). Australia's only native rhododendron, *Rhododendron lochae*, occurs on these windy cloud-clad summits. Between 800 and 1300 metres this rainforest type is referred to as Microphyll Vine-fern Forest, and at even higher altitudes as Microphyll Vine-fern Thicket.

When entering a tropical rainforest one is immediately struck by the marked change in climate within, where it is noticeably cooler, damper and darker. The overshadowing, interlocking, leafy branches of the canopy provide and maintain a humid and damp interior in which plant and animal life flourishes in great abundance and diversity. The forest canopy intercepts both sun and rain and, as a result, the forest floor, understorey and canopy have different micro-climates. The forest floor is still, gloomy and humid and the temperature varies little. At the top of the canopy there is strong sun, plenty of wind, and much daily variation in humidity and temperature. The diversity of plant and animal life is far richer than that of other terrestrial habitats and many of the plants and animals are highly adapted to life in the different levels, or strata, of the forest; such as in or around creeks and waterfalls, on the forest floor, in the understorey, or high up in the canopy.

Creeks and Waterfalls

The relative humidity within rainforest often reaches saturation point during the wet season. Swirling clouds of mist add to the extreme dampness. Perhaps less than half the rain that falls actually penetrates directly through the canopy to the forest floor. Below the canopy the rain is absorbed directly by tree bark and some epiphytic structures; some evaporates, whilst the remainder does eventually reach the forest floor via innumerable plants. Some rainforest trees have evolved 'drip-tips' at the end of their leaves to channel off excess moisture during rain and heavy mist. Excess water drains off down into mountain gullies, and into creeks to eventually cascade over waterfalls (**opposite**) and flow into lowland rivers and onwards to the sea.

Delicate filmy ferns, fan ferns and maiden veil ferns are particularly abundant in the damper environments of sheltered gullies and along creek banks (**right**). Some, such as the Giant or King Ferns and Potato Ferns, have long fronds, reaching a length of four metres or more. Umbrella-shaped tree fern crowns (**page i**) are formed by fronds that radiate out, in order to receive maximum light. The underside of each fern frond at times bears thousands of small spores. A spore germinates in favourable damp conditions to form a tiny heart-shaped structure called a prothallus. It is this that then produces the egg and sperm cells that eventually fuse to give rise to the fern plant as we know it. Many other plants, such as sundews, rock violets and weevil-lilies, also thrive in damp micro-environments.

A host of animals rely on moisture not just to drink or bathe in, or to reproduce in as frogs do, but possibly also for food. Within the water itself are myriads of micro-organisms, water insects and their larvae, yabbies or freshwater crayfish, tadpoles, eels, colourful fishes, and turtles. Platypuses burrow into creek and pool banks, usually under a protective tangle of roots. Although they are mostly active at dusk or dawn they may be glimpsed during the day paddling around a deeper pool and snapping up large prey or sifting through mud and extracting invertebrates that the touch and electro-sensitive bill detects. The vibrant blue plumage of an Azure Kingfisher (see page 47) may reveal the bird's presence on a nearby rock or branch. An Eastern Water Dragon (see page 32) may occasionally be glimpsed sunning itself on a rock or overhanging branch above cascading waters.

Frogs congregate to mate during the breeding season. Northern Great Barred Frogs (see page 28) visit water only to breed, spending the rest of their time in damp situations throughout the forest floor. Torrent Tree Frogs (see page 28), however, remain close to fast-flowing creeks. Immediately after heavy spring and summer rains male Orange-thighed Tree Frogs (see page 29) quickly congregate in low shrubs and grasses and commence calling loudly. Often other frogs and crickets join in the nocturnal chorus. It is most important that frogs keep moist, for they breathe through their skin as well as their nostrils. During the day they seek out moist refuges, such as under fallen logs or amongst the deeper warmer layers of leaf litter on the forest floor; or beneath litter accumulated by large epiphytic ferns in the understorey and canopy.

Mt. Lewis

Atherton Tableland

Forest Floor

Old leaves flutter down from the canopy, through the understorey, to the forest floor. Ripe fruits fall, rotten branches snap off and crash to the ground and ancient or diseased trees topple over and smash down other vegetation in their wake. Mosses of all shades of green soon blanket fallen trunks and as the trunks start to rot bracket-shaped fungal fruiting bodies grow from them (**right**). Each fungal fruiting body contains millions of microscopic single-celled reproductive spores, the equivalent of seeds in flowering plants, which, when mature, are dispersed by wind, rain-splash, animals or by the fruiting bodies themselves exploding. Although many of these fruit bodies resemble the familiar mushroom, some take on quite bizarre shapes, resembling corals, staghorns, shells, tongues or slime. Their, often quite vivid, red, yellow, orange, purple or blue hues add bright splashes of colour to the forest floor. Some even luminesce at night!.

Unlike most plants, fungi lack the green pigment chlorophyll, and so are unable to carry out photsynethesis; the means by which green plants manufacture food from carbon dioxide and water using energy from the sun's rays by a series of chemical reactions in their chlorophyll. Forest floor fungi feed as saprophytes. That is, they absorb food from dead and decaying plant and animal matter only. The main body of the fungus, concealed within the soil or wood substrate, is called a mycelium and consists of masses of fine threads called hyphae. Hyphae spread out over, or within, a rotting substrate such as leaves, logs or diseased trees, and from their tips secrete digestive enzymes which break down the dead plant material.

The Maiden Veil Fungus *Dictyophora indusiata* (**right**) belongs to a group of fungi called stinkhorns, on account of the terrible smell they emit. They require a substrate with a high organic and moisture content. The white phallus-shaped fruit body, some twenty centimetres high, emerges from the ground during the night and spreads its lacy veil. Almost immediately flies are attracted to the foetid slime that exudes from the stinkhorn cap. Landing on the lacy veil flies walk upwards onto the cap where they feed on the foul slime. The fungal spores stick to feet or mouthparts of the flies and are so dispersed. The following day the veil collapses and the fruit body of the fungus dies.

Fungi, and bacteria, are the instigators of the decomposition process. By breaking up the rotting vegetation into smaller bits and pieces, called detritus, they make available food for numerous small creatures collectively called detritivores – the next link in the complex forest floor food web. Worms, springtails, amphipods, mites, millipedes and snails live within leaf litter and surface soil layers and graze upon small bits of detritus, so breaking it down further. Leaf skeletons are common on the forest floor and these clearly indicate that the nutritious soft, once green, parts of the leaf have been digested away, not only by bacterial and fungal decomposers but also by the small detritivores, leaving only the less nutritious and digestible skeletons. Rainforest cockroaches and many beetles and their larvae feed directly upon rotting wood, and so further speed the breakdown process.

It is hard for us to imagine the microcosm of life that exists beneath our feet as we walk over the forest floor – billions of micro-organisms in each hectare of rainforest, playing one of the most significant roles within the tropical rainforest ecosystem. Whilst obtaining their own nourishment, the decomposers and the detritivores release from dead plant material the all-important nutrients in the form of their own body waste and, when they die, their own bodies. The nutrients released into the soil are then re-cycled by tree roots which absorb them for new plant growth.

Most plant roots grow just beneath, or on, the floor of the forest where nutrients are concentrated. In the soil conditions of tropical rainforest shallow roots are more efficient than are the deep root systems more commonly found in other habitats. Shallow root systems extend out horizontally either directly from the trunk base or from buttresses at the base of the tree. Buttresses are a striking feature of some rainforest trees (**left below**), and comprise woody flanged extensions radiating outwards from the lower part of the tree base. These structures may reach enormous proportions around the base of a rainforest giant and may be as tall as ten metres. Although buttresses to some extent support a tree's weight in shallow soils, by taking up strains and stresses, the functions of buttresses are not fully understood.

The intricate and balanced food web continues on the surface of the forest floor. Litter-dwelling carnivorous invertebrates, such as peripatus (see page 22), scorpions, pseudoscorpions, spiders, centipedes, beetles and other insects and their larvae, feed by hunting tiny detritivores. These in turn are food for larger ground-dwelling carnivores such as frogs, skinks, birds and mammals. The larger, warm-blooded, animals provide food for blood-sucking leeches.

During the day, chowchillas, whipbirds, scrubwrens, fernwrens and robins search systematically on and through leaf litter for small invertebrates. The lively and colourful Noisy Pitta (see page 47) eats insects, worms, leeches and snails, as well as eating fruit occasionally. The familiar Australian Brush-turkey (see page 39) and the delightful little Musky-rat Kangaroo (see page 66) are also omnivorous, eating both animals and fruits. At night bandicoots nose their way through litter and rotting logs for tasty grubs; native rats scurry about searching for fruits and small invertebrates; and dingoes lurk quietly within the forest gloom stalking suitable prey, which may even include the odd prickly Echidna.

Some forest floor animals eat fallen fruits and in so doing play a major role in the dispersal of plants. Fruits, such as those of the Blue Quandong, *Elaeocarpus angustifolius* (**left above**), are large, brightly coloured and highly edible. They are eaten in abundance by the mighty Southern Cassowary (see page 38). On the forest floor seeds germinate into delicate seedlings (**left**) which struggle for survival, and which compete with each other for light, space and nutrients. Some fall victim to browsing macropods such as the Red-legged Pademelon (see page 66). Successful seedlings grow into saplings and continue on, ever-upwards, into the next forest strata – the understorey.

The Understorey

This forest strata, between forest floor and canopy, supports an immense wealth of plant life, not just rainforest trees but many other plants. These include ground ferns, tree ferns, zamias, cunjevois, cordylines or palm-lilies, native gingers, native bananas, palms, climbing plants and epiphytes.

Many species of native gingers live within wet tropical rainforests where they favour moist shady situations. A most unusual ginger is the lowland-dwelling Native Torch Ginger, *Tapeinocheilos ananassae* (**right**). Its stem, which may be three metres high, bears large hard pointed leaves. It is sometimes called the Backscratcher Ginger because of the shape of its brilliant crimson inflorescence which consists of waxy rigid bracts each bearing a tubular yellow flower within.

Another strange plant is the Stinging Shrub, *Dendrocnide moroides* (**right below**). These shrubs favour more open and usually disturbed and sunnier areas of tropical forest and are, therefore, common along tracks. The leaves and the stems of the shrub are covered by stiff hairs which, if touched, inflict a painful sting. The plant manufactures its 'hairs' from mineral silica, the chief constituent of glass. If one is unlucky enough to brush against these hairs their tips penetrate the skin, break off, and an irritant poison is released. The effect of the sting may last for months. Even today there is no effective antidote, and visitors to tropical rainforests should be aware of stinging shrubs at all times. The hairs do not appear to sting some animals. Two species of beetle and the caterpillars of the White Nymph butterfly feed on the leaves; and the raspberry-like fruits are eaten by Spotted Catbirds (see page 57) and some other birds.

Epiphytes such as lichens, mosses, ferns and orchids, use trees for attachment purposes only and do not harm their supporting host in any way. Epiphytic roots absorb moisture from rainwater as it trickles down the tree trunks, and absorb nutrients from rotting vegetation trapped by the epiphytic structure itself, or from crevices in the bark of the supporting tree. Larger tree branches and trunks of the understorey, and the lower part of the canopy, support many epiphytic ferns, such as the Bird's or Crow's Nest, *Asplenium* species (**opposite**), Elkhorn, Staghorn and Basket Ferns. These basket-shaped epiphytes may reach massive proportions and provide an excellent catchment area for falling leaves and other plant debris. This rotting plant material not only provides these ferns with nutrients but also supports a miniature community of typically forest floor dwelling litter life. Insects and other small creatures thrive in these damp aerial micro-habitats and frogs and reptiles often shelter within the epiphytic foliage. It is not unusual to see normally ground-dwelling Eastern Whipbirds (see page 52) searching for food amongst the epiphytes, because here they find a diminutive 'forest floor' up in the air! Birds, such as Victoria's Riflebirds and Spotted Catbirds (see page 57), may build their nests upon or within epiphytes.

The greatest abundance and diversity of epiphytic ferns are found in tropical rainforests in high rainfall and cloudy areas. Some are adapted to grow in open sunnier areas, but most favour shady situations beneath the canopy.

Mt Spec National Park, Paluma

Lowland forest, Mission Beach

Whereas a few species of rainforest orchids are terrestrial and grow in shady conditions on the forest floor, most grow as epiphytes in the understorey or canopy where sufficient light penetrates for their growth. The diversity of orchids in the rainforests of the Wet Tropics is great. Some one hundred and fifty species have been recorded here and at least a quarter of them are peculiar, or endemic, to the area. Orchids display intricate and often brightly coloured flowers in order to attract suitable insect pollinators such as wasps, bees, moths or butterflies. The basic structure of all orchid flowers is similar, with three outer sepals and three inner petals. One petal is usually quite large and acts as a landing platform for the plant's insect pollinator. Some flowers even mimic the shape of their specific pollinator in order to attract them to their nectar and so ensure pollination. Some of the most commonly seen orchids of our tropical rainforests belong to the genus *Dendrobium*. This group includes spectacular orchids such as the familiar King and Pencil Orchids. The species illustrated here, *Dendrobium adae*, is only found in the upland forests of the Wet Tropics. Its lovely whitish-cream flowers (**left**) are waxy and fragrant. It is found in small clumps on trunks or larger branches.

The hundreds of tree trunks that one sees in the understorey are represented by all shapes, sizes and colours. Epiphytic lichens and mosses decorate the bark with hues of greens and yellows giving it a mottled and delicately textured appearance. Some trunks are quite smooth, others ridged or furrowed, whilst some, such as those of the Bumpy Satinash *Syzygium cormiflorum*, are conspicuously bumpy. Flowers (**left below**), and the subsequent fruits (**opposite**), grow from these woody bumps. Several species of rainforest trees exhibit this peculiar phenomenon, called cauliflory, in which flowers and fruits develop from the trunk or larger boughs. These cauliflorous trees, especially the smaller ones that are unable to reach the light and space of the upper canopy, display their flowers to understorey pollinators such as shade-loving butterflies and moths. During the daytime the delicate whitish nectar-rich blooms of the Bumpy Satinash attract such birds as honeyeaters and lorikeets whilst at night they may be visited by the Long-tailed Pygmy-possum (see page 64). Fruits of the Cluster Fig are also cauliflorous, growing from the trunk or older branches. These figs are eaten by the Double-eyed Fig-parrot (see page 42) and the Spectacled Flying-fox (see page 67).

Many species of palm trees occur in wet tropical rainforests including the Alexandra Palm, and several are endemic. The Atherton Palm is peculiar to the rainforests on mountain ranges above 800 metres in altitude, and the majestic palm *Oraniopsis appendiculata* is only found in upland areas of dense rainforests between the Big Tableland southward to inland of Innisfail where it grows in creek beds (**page 3**) or on slopes above streams. It is usually solitary and has a fairly stout trunk with a large crown of spreading fronds which may reach four metres in length. The splendid Fan Palm, *Licuala ramsayi* (**opposite**), is typical of lowland rainforests around Cape Tribulation (see page 7) and Mission Beach. It is a tall, slender palm with a spectacular crown of fan-shaped leaves.

15

Not all palms are trees with large woody trunks. Several of them, such as Lawyer Cane or Wait-a-While *Calamus motii*, have become climbers and form dense, often impenetrable, thickets along rainforest margins, creeks, tracks, roads and beneath breaks in the canopy (**page 6**). Long wiry stems with recurved hooks grow out and upward from axils of the leaves and function like grappling hooks as a climbing aid. These sharp hooks latch onto nearby vegetation and so support the palm as it grows upwards towards the light. The stem and main leaf axis of Lawyer Cane are armed with viciously sharp thorns (**right**) which certainly deter browsing animals from eating them. Many small birds, such as the Pale-yellow and Grey-headed Robins (see page 48), often build their nests amongst these dense vine tangles. The plant's protective armoury hinders climbing predators, such as the White-tailed Rat (see page 68), from stealing the eggs or chicks from the nest.

A great diversity of climbing plants live within the wet tropical rainforests. The seeds of climbing plants germinate on the forest floor. The successful seedlings grow upwards, supported by a host tree which they do not damage in any way, through the understorey and upward into the canopy to reach the energy-giving light that is imperative if the plants are to reach maturity. Some climbers, referred to as 'twiners', spiral or entwine their way up a host trunk into the canopy. Their stems may become thick and woody to form lianas (**opposite**). Having reached the canopy lianas then travel horizontally from tree crown to tree crown, often over great distances. Stems may reach massive proportions, some round and twisted and others wide and flattened.

Not all climbing plants are 'twiners' or use hooks like the climbing palms. Several species of rainforest-dwelling pandanus, or screw-pines as they are often referred to, have become climbers. The Climbing Pandanus, *Freycinetia excelsa*, attaches itself to a host tree with small lateral roots. These stem roots are small and numerous and closely hold the vine to the supporting tree. The main stem gives rise to many loosely hanging branches that may reach a metre in length. The male or female flowers develop at the end of a branch surrounded by bright orange leaf-like bracts the brilliant colouration of which attracts birds such as honeyeaters to the nectar supply and so ensure pollination. The succulent red Climbing Pandanus fruits (**right**) are eaten by pigeons, honeyeaters, riflebirds and bowerbirds. The Native Monstera and the Pepper Vine are also root climbers whilst the Supplejack Vine has spring-like prehensile tendrils on its leaf tips for coiling around a suitable support.

The diverse and complex plant life in the understorey supports a multitude of animals. Moths, butterflies, bees, ants, flies, preying mantids, stick insects, beetles, crickets, cicadas and spiders are just some of the numerous and abundant understorey invertebrates. They are preyed upon by skinks, geckoes and monitors; and by birds such as robins, fantails, scrubwrens, gerygones, shrike-thrushes and treecreepers. Many species of frugivorous birds, such as some pigeons and bowerbirds, build their nests in well protected sites amongst the understorey, but these birds forage mostly on fruits in the next forest strata – the canopy.

Dunk Island

Mt Spec National Park, Paluma

The Canopy

Interlocking tree crowns (**page ii**) clad at times with beautiful flowers and colourful succulent fruits, supporting an arboreal garden of tangled vines, mosses, lichens, orchids, mistletoes, giant elkhorn and bird's nest ferns, constitute the rainforest canopy. The canopy may be even or uneven (with several layers of trees) and may be as high as forty five metres above the floor. Giant emergent trees reach more impressive heights projecting well above the canopy level and spreading their massive crowns over it. Leaves vary in size, shape, texture and colour (**page iii**). Delicate young leaves may be red due to a pigment called anthocyanin which may make the leaves distasteful to some animals that would otherwise eat them. Leaves of some tree species are eaten by ringtail possums or tree kangaroos.

Rainforest fruits are also an important food source for many of the fruit and seed-eating canopy-dwelling animals, who in turn act as important dispersal agents for the trees. The outer fruit case, or pericarp, may be soft and succulent or hard and woody and may enclose one or many seeds. Succulent fruits are eaten by fruit-eating pigeons, bowerbirds and flying-foxes, whereas harder woody nuts and seeds are favoured by parrots.

The succulent fruits of strangler figs, such as those of *Ficus destruens* (**left**), are eaten by many species of fruit-eating birds. The indigestible seeds are then voided by the birds and these will germinate in some tree crevice or hole. The young fig starts its life as an epiphyte in the canopy, or understorey, unlike other tree seedlings that have to start their struggle for survival on the forest floor. It grows slowly at first, for there is little water or food for it, but its leathery leaves reduce water loss. Eventually it puts out long cable-like roots that descend down the host tree trunk to the forest floor and root into the soil beneath it. Now it can readily absorb nutrients and water and the young fig tree flourishes. The thin roots become thicker and interlace their way tightly around the supporting host tree trunk. The expanding leafy crown of the strangler starts to shade the crown of the support tree and its roots start to strangle the host. The host tree slowly rots away leaving a totally independent strangler fig (**opposite**) which may live for several hundred years or more. Most famous of all individual fig trees in the Wet Tropics are the 'Curtain' and 'Cathedral' figs, which can be seen on the Atherton Tableland. These fig trees, called White or Deciduous Figs, are massive and most of their roots, instead of encircling the host's trunk, hang vertically downwards in a free-fall to the forest floor to create a curtain-like structure.

Mistletoes, like Strangler Figs, start life up in the canopy. Mistletoes are partial parasites, that is they derive their water and nutrients from the host tree to its detriment, but their green leaves carry out photosynthesis, as do all green plants, to produce additional foods. Mistletoes have evolved a fascinating way of ensuring the dispersal of their fruits. Mistletoebirds and other frugivores eat the soft mistletoe berries. The seeds within are sticky and when voided adhere to a branch and germinate there. Many of the rainforest mistletoes, such as *Dendrophthoe falcata* (**left**), have spectacular large red flowers.

19

Canopy flowers often provide a contrasting splash of colour against their dense leafy green background. They vary considerably in colour, shape, size and scents and are designed to attract nectar-feeding canopy-dwellers in order to ensure their pollination. Butterflies, bees, lorikeets, honeyeaters and others feed on nectar-yielding flowers during the day and in doing so act as important pollinators. At night moths, blossom bats, flying-foxes, and, in the uplands, the Long-tailed Pygmy-possum (see page 64), fill this important role. Some honeyeaters, such as the Eastern Spinebill, have a long thin tapering bill which can probe deep down into tubular-shaped flowers. The bill of the Yellow-spotted Honeyeater (see page 55) is, however, much stouter and this bird, like the broad-tongued lorikeets and blossom bats, favours more open flowers.

The Proteaceae is one of the most significant plant families in the rainforests of the Wet Tropics, being represented here by approximately fifty species, of which about seventy percent are peculiar to the area. The family includes many popularly cultivated trees, such as the silky oaks, tree waratahs, and macadamias that are also grown commercially for their edible nuts.

Several species of silky oaks, such as the Northern Silky Oak, Brown Silky Oak and the Ivory Curl Flower, are endemic to the wet tropical rainforests. The extremely durable wood of these silky oaks, particularly that of the Northern Silky Oak, was once of major value to the timber industry. These magnificent trees may reach a height of some thirty metres and have dense crowns of large leaves which bear clusters of creamy nectar-rich fragrant flowers borne on long spikes. The photograph (**right above**) shows a Common Jezabel butterfly (see page 26) sipping nectar from the flowers of the Brown Silky Oak, *Darlingia darlingiana*.

The Pink-flowered Euodia, *Euodia elleryana* (family Rutaceae), occurs predominantly in coastal riverine rainforests. In summer it produces spectacular clusters of fragrant, pinkish-mauve flowers which attract many nectar-feeding honeyeaters and lorikeets, such as the Scaly-breasted Lorikeet (**right**). Many colourful butterflies are also attracted to the flowers, including the spectacular Ulysses Butterfly which utilizes the leaves as an important food plant for its larvae (see page 26). This highly ornamental tree is popularly grown in gardens and parks.

The Umbrella Tree, *Schefflera actinophylla* (family Araliaceae), needs little introduction as it is widely cultivated in tropical and sub-tropical gardens. The flowers are bright red and are borne on groups of long spikes that radiate out from the end of each branch and provide a rich nectar source for honeyeaters and lorikeets, such as the Rainbow Lorikeet (**opposite above**). Umbrella Trees sometimes grow as epiphytes high up in the canopy.

The Black Bean, *Castanospermum australe* (family Fabaceae), is also a familiar tree to many people, as it is decorative and widespread in rainforests from north-eastern Queensland to north-eastern New South Wales. Its brilliant red or yellowish flowers (**opposite below**) are quite spectacular and are nectar-rich and utilised by many of the canopy-dwelling nectar feeders. The large pendulous woody pods enclose brown chestnut-like seeds.

21

INVERTEBRATES

An amazing diversity of invertebrates lives in the rainforests of the Wet Tropics. Leeches, worms, amphipods, beetles, ants, pseudoscorpions, scorpions, centipedes, millipedes, mites, ticks, spiders and snails live amongst leaf litter, under logs or on trunks; moths, butterflies, cicadas, bees and wasps fly around the understorey and canopy; and myriads of microscopic invertebrates, water insects and yabbies flourish in pools and creeks. The exact number of species is unknown but during a recent survey some five thousand species of insects and three hundred species of spiders were identified from the Russell River in the lowlands to the summit of the Bellenden Ker Range (see map, page 71).

Tiger Leech

Lurking amongst litter or foliage is the much-feared, but usually quite harmless, rainforest-dwelling leech (**right**). It has one large sucker surrounding the mouth and another at the posterior end, and both are used for locomotion. Using these suckers it loops its way around the forest floor and foliage in search of a suitable host, such as a bird or wallaby. Small receptor organs in the skin can detect light and dark, heat and cold and can possibly also detect body odours and blood. The mouth houses two small jaws, each equipped with tiny sharp teeth that pierce the victim's skin. An anti-coagulant in the leech saliva prevents blood from clotting. A leech can ingest up to ten times its body weight in blood.

Peripatus
Peripatoides species

The caterpillar-like Peripatus, or Velvet Worm as it is sometimes called (**right**), is interesting because it exhibits features that are intermediate between two main animal groups, namely the worms and the joint-legged animals, or arthropods (such as insects, millipedes and centipedes). The ancestors of peripatus moved from sea to land about four hundred million years ago and today peripatus are still found on most of the land masses derived from ancient Gondwanaland. These 'living fossils' are voracious little carnivores and have a deadly way of attacking prey, such as a cricket or beetle. They eject jets of glue-like slime from the blunt papillae on either side of their head which, like superglue, hardens immediately and immobilises the victim!

River Crayfish
Euastacus fleckeri

Most people are familiar with freshwater crayfish or yabbies. The large and spectacular bright blue and red River Crayfish (**opposite**, and lower right of front cover) is only found in the mountain streams of the Mount Lewis area. It is a scavenger, feeding mainly on detritus. Its two large formidable-looking pincers are used in aggressive combat against rivals.

Atlas Moth
Coscinocera hercules

The spectacular Atlas or Hercules Moth belongs to the family Saturniidae. It is the largest Australian species and one of the largest moths on earth. It only occurs in tropical rainforests of north-eastern Queensland and New Guinea. Males (**right**) are slightly smaller than females, which can have a wing span of about twenty five centimetres, and differ from them in having much longer feather-like antenna and more tapering tail-like hind wings. Females secrete chemicals to attract males which detect the females' scent with their long antennae. After mating, a female lays some eighty to one hundred eggs on the leaves or stems of six to eight rainforest tree species, which represent the caterpillars' only food plants. Sadly, females die shortly after mating and egg laying, as they have no mouth parts and so are unable to feed. They can only live as long as their fat deposits last. The blue-green caterpillars grow to some ten centimetres long before they spin cocoons and pupate.

A bewildering variety of moths, such as Hawk Moths, Emperor Gum Moths, Grass Moths, Tiger Moths and Dayflying Moths, occur in the wet tropical rainforests. They range in size from very small to large and some are exquisitely patterned and brightly coloured. Most moths feed on flower nectar and play an important role as rainforest plant pollinators. Other moths seek out the juices of ripe fruit. Some of the fruit-sucking species have leaf-like upper wings mottled in shades of brown to blend in with the undergrowth or bark and so conceal them from predators. When disturbed, however, they immediately flash open their upper wings to reveal brilliantly coloured hind wings which may frighten off predators. Some moths are orange and black in colour and resemble wasps. By mimicking an unpalatable insect, such as a wasp, they avoid predation.

Zodiac Moth
Alcides zodiaca

This large and most attractive moth (**right**), belonging to the family Uraniidae, resembles a swallowtail butterfly. Like most butterflies, it is diurnal and can be commonly seen flitting about during the day or sipping nectar from rainforest flowers with its long proboscis. Late in the day it often soars back and forth above the canopy. It can be recognised as a moth because it rests with its wings outspread, quite unlike butterflies which hold their wings together above their bodies most of the time. The larvae of this moth feed predominantly on the leaves of a large vine, *Omphalea queenslandiae*, and they pupate in thin transparent cocoons between dead leaves on the ground or in crevices.

The closely related and larger brownish-black White-striped Moth also resembles a swallowtail butterfly. It is nocturnal and is usually only seen when it turns up at household lights at night. Although relatively rare in these rainforests, it is much more common in New Guinea and south-eastern Asia.

 Regent Skipper
Euschemon rafflesia

The most important resource for butterflies is their larval food plant and for most that means foliage, flowers or fruits of living plants. The abundance and diversity of this resource helps account for the numbers of butterflies evident in northern tropical rainforests. There are some three hundred and eighty five species of butterflies in Australia. Of this total approximately seventy five species occur within the rainforest of the Wet Tropics. These butterflies include the skippers (family Hesperiidae), swallowtails (Papilionidae), whites and yellows (Pieridae), browns and nymphs (Nymphalidae) and small blues and spectacular jewels (Lycaenidae).

The Regent Skipper belongs to the skipper family, the Hesperiidae. The immaculate magnificent adult of this species is shown here (**left**) soon after emerging from its pupa. When resting, especially in sunlight, the adults open their wings almost flat. Adult Regent Skippers usually fly within the rainforest and are frequently seen taking nectar from blossom. Females may be encountered diligently searching for their larval food plant, which they usually fly around several times before selecting a site at which to lay an egg. The spectacularly marked larvae feed on the foliage of understorey shrubs.

The Regent Skipper is of special interest to science for it is perhaps the most primitive of the world's butterflies and represents an important link between moths and butterflies. One of the distinguishing features between butterflies and moths is that the latter possess an organ, called a frenulum, which locks the fore and hind wings together during flight. Butterflies do not have these. The single exception to this rule is the male Regent Skipper (females are more advanced as they have lost theirs!).

Other members of the skipper family occurring in these rainforests include the Black Skipper, Black and White Swift, the Black and White Flat, the Banded Demon and the rare Purple Brown-eye.

 Helena Brown
Tisiphone helena

This fairly large handsome brown butterfly (**left**) is unique to the upland rainforests of the Wet Tropics. The close relatives of this species occur in southern Australia. Despite the more uniform climate of the tropics adult Helena Browns have retained a strong seasonality and are on the wing in summer only. It is common to see them flying in and out of the forest amongst the clumps of sword-grass upon which their larvae feed.

The family Nymphalidae, to which the Helena Brown belongs, includes many rainforest-dwelling species such as the Australian Lurcher, Cruiser, Australian Leafwing, Australian Vagrant, Red Lacewing, Blue-banded Eggfly, Hamadryad and White Nymph. Interestingly, the larvae of the White Nymph butterfly feed gregariously underneath the leaf of the Stinging Shrub (see page 12).

Grey Albatross
Appias melania

The Grey Albatross is confined to the Wet Tropics where it is often seen along the edge of rainforest feeding on flowers, including those of the troublesome invader *Lantana* (**right**). This weed is an introduced species, of South American origin, that grows so quickly and efficiently that it has become a major pest in disturbed areas of rainforest. Its brightly coloured pink, red, orange and yellow flowers are nectar-rich and attract a lot of the rainforest-dwelling butterflies, including the Ulysses and Birdwing (see below).

The Grey Albatross belongs to the family Pieridae which also includes Nysa Jezabel, Nigidius Jezabel, Union Jack and Common Jezabel (**page 20**).

Birdwing Butterfly
Ornithoptera priamus

The Birdwing Butterfly, of the family Papilionidae, is one of the largest and most handsome of all Australian butterflies and is strongly sexually dimorphic. The male is richly coloured in green, gold and black (**opposite above**). The larger female, with a wing span of up to twenty centimetres, is black and white with yellow markings on the hindwings; and is shown here drying her wings after emerging from the pupa (**opposite below**). Males sometimes set up a territory near the larval food plant, the vigorous large-leaved vine *Aristolochia tagala*, and in the early morning patrol around its base in search of freshly-emerging females. These may be mated just after they have emerged from a pupa, and before their wings are dry, and often two or three males are seen trying to mate with a single female.

There can be few sights as spectacular as a soaring Birdwing Butterfly gliding amongst the foliage or sweeping down to take nectar from a flower. Writing in 1856, the great naturalist Alfred Wallace described his joy at seeing a birdwing during his sojourn in the Malay Archipelago. To him *Ornithoptera* were the 'largest most perfect and beautiful of butterflies'.

Other species of papilionids that occur in tropical rainforests include the Blue Triangle, Green-spotted Triangle, Macleay's Swallowtail, Ambrax Butterfly, Capaneus Butterfly and Ulysses Butterfly.

Ulysses Butterfly
Papilio ulysses

This exquisite butterfly (**right**) is widely used as a symbol of tourism throughout tropical north-eastern Queensland. Its brilliant metallic blue upperwings, edged with velvety black, contrast strikingly with the brownish cryptic markings of its underwings. The Ulysses Butterfly is commonly seen at lookouts soaring above the canopy or moving in and out of foliage with the blue appearing to flash on and off as the wings rapidly open and close. The underside is cryptic when the butterfly is at rest. Larvae feed on leaves of the rainforest tree *Euodia elleryana* (see page 20).

FROGS

There are about two hundred species of frogs in Australia. Of this total twenty three species occur in the rainforests of the Wet Tropics, and all but two of them are peculiar to the area.

The largest Australian family is the Myobatrachidae, a mixed bag of about one hundred species confined to Australia and New Guinea. Most are uniquely Australian frogs and three species (see below) are endemic to the wet tropical rainforests. There are some seventy one species of tree frogs belonging to the family Hylidae in Australia. Eight of these, belonging to the genera *Litoria* (seven species) and *Nyctimystes* (one species), occur in these rainforests, and six of them are endemic. Twelve of the sixteen species of truly tropical frogs, belonging to the Microhylidae, occur in the rainforests of the wet tropics and all of them are endemic.

Several other species of frogs are often encountered in wet tropical rainforests, but are not dependent upon them. They also occur in other habitats and appear to use rainforest only as a refuge during very dry conditions. These include the magnificent Giant Tree Frog and the Wood Frog, the only 'true' frog in Australia, of the family Ranidae. Unfortunately the introduced Cane Toad has successfully invaded tropical rainforests with tracks and roadways.

Frog measurements given for each species are for snout to vent (cloaca) length.

Northern Barred Frog
Mixophyes schevilli

The impressive Northern Barred Frog, *Mixophyes schevilli* (**right above**), belonging to the family Myobatrachidae, is endemic to the wet tropical rainforests. It is large, with powerful long legs and well webbed feet, and lives amongst litter on the forest floor. Its call note, a deep resonant *wahk*, is mostly heard during wet weather and close to streams. The average size of this frog is ninety millimetres, but some individuals may reach one hundred and ten millimetres. Two other members of this family, belonging to the genus *Taudactylus*, are also endemic in this area.

Torrent Tree Frog
Litoria nannotis

The Torrent Tree Frog (**right**), or Waterfall Frog as it is sometimes called, is beautifully adapted to life on wet moss and algae-covered rocks within and adjacent to waterfalls and torrents. Colouration varies from olive green to brown to almost blackish, in order to harmonize with rock colouration of its environment.

This sixty five millimetre long frog leaps from potential trouble into torrential white water to disappear. It permits itself to be swept downstream before emerging onto another wet rock where it remains motionless to avoid detection.

Orange-thighed Tree Frog
Litoria xanthomera

As can be seen from its photograph (**left**, and lower left of front cover) this is one of the most strikingly beautiful of the tree frogs, due to a pleasing combination of bright greens, yellows, and red. It is more often than not heard rather than seen. Immediately after heavy spring and summer rains individuals quickly congregate in low shrubs and grasses and commence their loud choruses. In these brief nocturnal gatherings they continuously emit long repetitious growls or 'moans' which slowly increase in volume before being followed by a lovely soft series of trills. These vocalisations are accompanied by an impressive inflation of the yellow vocal sac which is presumably also a visual display. Toe pads on the tip of each digit, so typical of the tree frog family, are effectively 'sucker pads' much assisting these frogs to climb. This is a frog of sixty five millimetre average adult length.

This tree frog used to be known to scientists as the Red-eyed Tree Frog, *Litoria chloris*, and was thought to range down the Australian east coastal zone from about Cooktown in Queensland to central New South Wales. It was shown in 1986, however, that the northern population of this frog, restricted to the Wet Tropics, is a previously overlooked new species *Litoria xanthomera*.

Green-eyed Frog
Litoria genimaculata

The Green-eyed Frog (**left**) is usually found close to streams and seepages associated with damp mosses and lichens, but is also found on the forest floor and on trees. The appearance of this frog has evolved to closely match its microhabitat, with colours and shapes that make it extremely cryptic. It has even developed rows of small pieces of skin, or lappets, along the edge of the limbs which effectively break-up the normal frog outline, or contours, making the animal more difficult to perceive.

The general colouration of this frog is variable, the basic body colour being a shade of brown, reddish-brown, or olive with irregular darker patches. There is usually a dark, or russet, large colour patch between the eyes. Perched upon a moss and lichen covered branch at the edge of a lushly vegetated creek this frog is very difficult to see. It grows to an average length of sixty five millimetres. Males are much smaller than females.

Eight species of the tree frog family, the Hylidae, occur in the wet tropical rainforests. The Green-eyed Frog and Lesueur's Frog are the only two tree frogs that occur in rainforests elsewhere, namely in southern Queensland and on Cape York Peninsula respectively. The other six species, including the Torrent Tree Frog (see opposite) and the Orange-thighed Tree Frog (see above), are endemic to this area.

REPTILES

Some seven hundred reptile species occur in Australia; two species of crocodiles, six species of marine turtles, seventeen species of tortoises, one hundred and sixty five snake species and over five hundred lizard species that include geckoes, legless lizards, monitors or goannas, dragon lizards and skinks. It is difficult to state the precise number of reptiles that occur in the rainforests of the Wet Tropics as new species, particularly of smaller skinks, are still being discovered and described. At present some twenty four reptile species are recognised as being confined to, or have a large part of their distribution in, the rainforests of the Wet Tropics. Eighteen species are endemic to this area and these include the Chameleon Gecko, Boyd's Forest Dragon, one species of *Cacophis* snake and fifteen species of skinks. The Leaf-tailed Gecko, two species of skinks, the Amethystine Python, the Rough-scaled Snake and the Black-bellied Swamp Snake occur in this area and elsewhere in Australia.

Several other reptile species occur in tropical rainforests but are not dependent upon them and are just as common, if not more so, in other habitats. These include the Eastern Water Dragon, Spotted Tree Monitor, Carpet Python, Red-bellied Black Snake and the Brown, Northern and Common Tree Snakes. Several species of freshwater tortoises occur in rainforested creeks, lagoons and pools and the Estuarine Crocodile frequents larger rivers, such as the Daintree.

Estuarine Crocodile
Crocodylus porosus

Visitors to the Wet Tropics should be aware of the possibility of encountering a crocodile if they are camping, fishing, boating or swimming in lowland rivers that flow through the rainforest. Large Estuarine Crocodiles are quite capable of killing and eating people that are careless enough to give them the opportunity! This awesome crocodile (**right above**) may attain a total length of over seven metres, but few individuals have been found larger than five metres long. It inhabits estuaries and may be seen swimming out at sea, but it also dwells in rivers, swamps, billabongs and pools well inland, which it reaches via river systems during periods of flood and also by limited overland excursions. It is largely nocturnal, and it feeds on crustaceans, fish, reptiles, birds and mammals.

Despite its fearsome appearance, it is a very delicate animal when nesting. Females scrape together a substantial mound of debris, vegetation and soil on a river or billabong bank with their feet, tail, and even the sides of the body. Once the nest is complete the female lays across the apex and digs an egg chamber with her hind legs. She then raises her hind quarters slightly to deposit her thirty to eighty white hard-shelled eggs and then covers them carefully with sensitive movements of her legs. She then retires to adjacent water to await their hatching. From here she will vigorously defend the nest and eggs from any disturbance. The female returns to the nest when the young can be heard giving their little yelping calls from the egg, and she will actually carry the hatchlings to water in her powerful toothy mouth!

Chameleon Gecko
Carphodactylus laevis

This spectacular gecko (**opposite below**) lives only in tropical rainforest, where it spends the daylight hours concealed beneath forest floor litter and ground debris. It is the only member of the genus *Carphodactylus* and only occurs in upland forest above 590 metres altitude, from the Big Tableland to the Cardwell Range. It forages at night upon the forest floor and over low vegetation, ground debris and tree trunks for small invertebrates such as crickets. It has a snout to vent length of some fourteen centimetres, and is made most distinctive by a conspicuous sharp ridge down the central back to the tail. The tail is a rich brown with white bands and is tapered at the end. When disturbed by a predator the gecko readily sheds its tail which, as a result of reflex muscle contractions, continues to wriggle and squeak. This not only provides the predator with a distracting tasty meal but, more typically, also allows the gecko to escape. It then grows a new tail which, unlike the original, is orange-brown with small dark blotches.

About eighty species belonging to the gecko family Gekkonidae occur in Australia. The Chameleon and Northern Leaf-tailed Geckoes are the only two that live predominantly in the rainforests of this region, and are considered relict and primitive species that possibly had ancient connections with Gondwanaland.

Northern Leaf-tailed Gecko
Phyllurus cornutus

This incredible looking gecko (**left**) is as large as any other gecko found in Australia, averaging sixteen centimetres in length. Some individuals attain an overall length of twenty five centimetres. It is a tree-dwelling nocturnal animal of sluggish movements that relies very much upon its remarkably cryptic appearance to avoid detection by predators. It may be found beneath loose tree bark or in tree crevices during the day, but is active on trees, rocks, and occassionally on the ground at night. This gecko has long thin clawed digits totally lacking the adhering toe discs of many gecko species. In this arboreal species clawed toes assist in climbing over rough surfaces. Females lay two soft shelled eggs.

Very few adults are found to still have their original tail and this is indicative of the fact that this gecko does have predatory enemies. Original tails are very spiky, like the rest of the animal, but regenerated tails are smooth (see photo). This gecko's predators include at least some owls, rats and snakes. Its original tail is similar in general shape to its head and when disturbed the gecko raises and moves the tail to attract attention to it and away from its head. If the predator then grasps the fatty tail the reptile is able to drop it and escape, whilst the released tail continues to thrash about for a brief time as a result of reflex muscle contractions.

Until recently the three distinctive populations of leaf-tailed geckoes in eastern Australian were considered to be of one species. It has recently been found, however, that at least the southernmost population represents a distinct species.

31

Boyd's Forest Dragon
Hypsilurus boydii

There are some sixty five species of dragon lizards, of the family Agamidae, in Australia and most of them are diurnal, terrestrial and inhabit drier parts of the continent. This extremely handsome dragon lizard (**right**) is, however, arboreal and occurs in the rainforests of the Wet Tropics. It is diurnal and feeds on insects, snails and slugs as well as soft fruits. At night it may retreat high into a tree. It grows to a length of fifteen centimetres, but the tail adds much to its overall length. Despite its ornate structures and bright colouration it is cryptic in its tropical rainforest environment, where it harmonizes well with the vegetation.

Eastern Water Dragon
Physignathus lesueurii

The Eastern Water Dragon is commonly seen in tropical rainforests basking in the sun on rock or overhanging branch above creeks. The tall spiked nuchal crest scales continue down the back and tail to give it a 'dragon-like' appearance (**right below**). It grows to twenty centimetres, with a strong long tail that grows to two and a half times the body length. The tail is compressed laterally as an aid to swimming, for this animal often plunges into water and swims away from danger. The placement of its nostrils right on top of its snout is an adaptation to aquatic habits.

Spotted Tree Monitor
Varanus timorensis

Monitors, or goannas as they are sometimes called, belong to the family Varanidae which in Australia consists of twenty five species. The Spotted Tree Monitor is an arboreal species that utilizes the shelter of hollow tree trunks as resting places. It hunts in trees and on the ground for insects, amphibians, reptiles and mammals. It rarely exceeds sixty to seventy centimetres in overall length. This monitor occurs through a wide range of habitats from wet tropical rainforests to drier areas. In drier habitats it is usually a paler grey with light markings. Darker colouration in rainforest (**opposite above**) is of course more appropriate for camouflage.

Burrowing Legless Skink
Coeranoscincus frontalis

The family Scincidae, represented by some two hundred and eighty seven species, is the largest lizard family in Australia. The Burrowing Skink (**opposite below**) is one of eleven legless or near legless burrowing skinks occurring in Australia. It is endemic to the rainforests of the Wet Tropics where it occurs mostly in upland areas above 600 metres altitude. It grows to a length of about twenty five centimetres and is brown or grey-blue above with a yellowish underside. It is to be found under logs, and leaf litter. It feeds on small leaf litter invertebrates, such as beetle larvae.

Northern Rainforest Skink
Eulamprus tigrinus

The exact number of skink species in this region is unknown, as new species are still being discovered and described. To date, however, some seventeen species are known to occur in these rainforests and fifteen of them, including this species (**right**) and the Prickly Forest Skink (see below), are endemic.

This attractive skink has to date lacked a common name, and so we suggest Northern Rainforest Skink be used. The rich tan-brown to orange-brown sides of the back are strongly striped with black markings that have earnt it the latin name *tigrinus*. It is endemic to the Wet Tropics, occurring mostly in mid-montane to upland rainforests from just south of Cooktown, to the Cardwell Ranges. It is often seen basking in sunlit patches of rainforest floor, on fallen trunks, or lower tree trunks, usually no more than one or two metres above ground. It climbs in search of prey, feeding upon insects such as crickets. It grows to about eight centimetres.

Prickly Forest Skink
Gnypetoscincus queenslandiae

The Prickly Forest Skink (**right below**) is endemic to the Wet Tropics, occurring in lowland and upland rainforests from the Big Tableland, just south of Cooktown, southward to the Cardwell Range. This skink may grow as long as nine and one half centimetres and, as its common name suggests, its body is very rough and prickly. During the day it rests in moist areas beneath rotting logs, well within the rainforest. It actively hunts at night for worms, insects and spiders.

Amethystine Python
Morelia amethistina

This python (**opposite**) is named for the lovely amethystine-like iridescence that can be seen on its scales when suitable light permits. It is the largest of Australia's fifteen species of pythons (family Boidae) and has been authentically recorded at eight and a half metres (twenty eight feet) long. In Australia this python occurs in the Wet Tropics and on Cape York Peninsula, but is also found in New Guinea where it inhabits wet tropical rainforests and also monsoon forests, scrubby vine forests and mangroves. The Amethystine Python preys upon fruit bats, possums, rats and pademelons; and also eats birds, particularly ground-frequenting species. Like most pythons it has a series of conspicuous pits along its jaws which house very efficient heat-sensitive organs which enable it to locate warm-blooded animals. It seizes prey with widely-gaping mouth lined with numerous backward-curving needle-sharp teeth, and then immediately throws coils of its body length around the prey to constrict and suffocate it.

A female python lays a clutch of between ten to twenty eggs that form a cohesive clump, and about which she coils herself to keep the eggs warm and protect them.

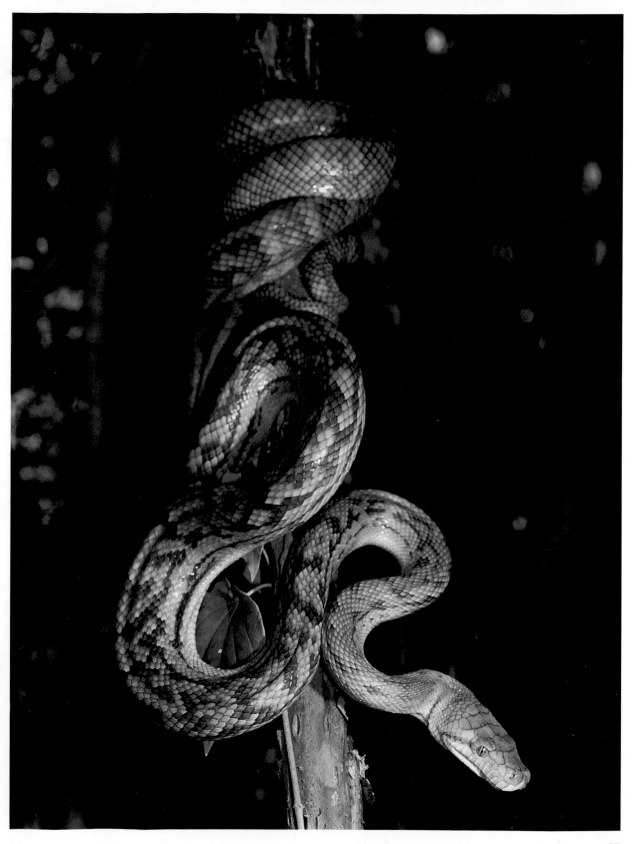

Carpet Python
Morelia spilota

By far our best known python is the Carpet, as it is commonly encountered throughout its distribution. It is found from wet tropical rainforests to very arid near-deserts of the interior; as well as occurring in New Guinea. It is variable in colour and pattern in different parts of its range. It grows to an adult length of about two metres, but some may attain four metres.

Whilst it is generally very similar to the Amethystine Python in appearance, the two can be distinguished by the head scales. Large tortoise-like scales adorn the top of the Amethystine's head whereas the Carpet Python is here covered with numerous small scales (**right**). The Carpet Python is more commonly found climbing in tree foliage than is the Amethystine, and is a crepuscular and nocturnal hunter, but may sun bask in any situation and be found active in daylight. Its prey consists of a range of mammals, birds and the occasional reptile.

Few people realize that the pythons still have remnants of hind legs, having evolved from legged ancestors. Either side of the vent, or anus, is a claw-like spur that is much more obvious in some species than in others. This is all that remains to be seen of the hind limbs in the present-day pythons. Clear evidence that these spurs are in fact vestigial limbs is supplied by the anatomy of the python skeleton, which exhibits all three parts of the pelvic bones required to connect to legs. As modern pythons no longer have legs and get about perfectly well without them they are clearly in the evolutionary process of loosing the bones associated with the, once better developed, limbs.

Black-bellied Swamp Snake
Hemiaspis signata

The northernmost population of this snake has been recorded from Thornton Peak southward to Mount Spec on the Paluma Range (see map, page 71), where it inhabits wet tropical rainforests and adjacent forest areas. The Black-bellied Swamp Snake (**right**) or Marsh or Swamp Snake, varies in basic upper body colour from russet or pinkish, in Queensland, to olive-brown to brown or blackish, with a usually slightly darker head. The attractive head markings are typical. The underside is cream, pinkish or dark grey to blackish. It is diurnal and eats skinks, frogs, and small snakes, but it may be active during warmer nights. This snake is about sixty centimetres long but larger individuals may attain a metre in length. It bears live young in litters of from four to twenty, with an average of eleven.

Australia is renowned for its large number of dangerously venomous snakes, belonging to the family Elapidae which includes the very dangerous Taipan and Brown Snakes. Although these front-fanged snakes are referred to collectively as dangerous, many species lack sufficiently potent venom or delivery mechanisms to be a threat to people. Large specimens of the Black-bellied Swamp Snake can deliver a most painful bite and several authors note that treatment should always be sought in the case of a child being bitten.

Red-bellied Black Snake
Pseudechis porphyriacus

The handsome Red-bellied Black Snake, belonging to the family Elapidae, is one of eastern Australias best known larger poisonous snakes. It is abundant in suitable habitats such as tropical rainforest where it is often seen basking at creek and track edges. The Red-bellied Black Snake is diurnal and usually closely associates with streams and other water, but may also be found well away from it. When not hunting or basking it may be found beneath timber, rocks or down holes and burrows. It has a varied diet, including frogs, snakes, lizards, birds, mammals and some fish. It is a jet black snake with a paler, brownish, snout. The common name describes the lovely red colour of its ventral scales, and the first row of adjacent lateral scales, as are clearly seen in the accompanying photograph. The underside of the tail is blackish. Adults average a length of about one and a half meters, but large specimens can attain two to two and a half metres.

Under normal circumstances this is a snake eager to avoid disturbance, and it is only when cornered that it will perform the photographed stance (**left**) as a last resort. Its fore-body is held ready to strike the photographer who is crowding it so that its underside might be shown. Even then it will usually throw only bluff strikes, without even opening the mouth. Whilst not considered a deadly snake a good bite from large specimens could be serious and should be immediately treated as such.

Rough-scaled Snake
Tropidechis carinatus

Tropical populations of the Rough-scaled Snake (**left**) are confined to rainforests and adjacent forests in the Wet Tropics, where they are usually associated with water. Rough-scaled Snakes are usually nocturnal, but may also be found basking or foraging for frog, lizard and small mammal prey during the day. Three quarters of a metre is about the average length of this snake, but individuals do grow to almost a metre. It varies in basic colour from an olive-brown, green or grey to dark brown, with indistinct dark grey or blackish cross bands. The underside may be cream, yellowish, or greenish. Its name describes the course texture of its body scales, the centre of which are strongly keeled.

This species of elapid snake is a potentially very dangerous one, more so than the Red-bellied Black Snake (see above), because its venom is particularly lethal and it has been noted as highly alert, nervous, aggressive and difficult to handle. Several people have died from its bite. It should perhaps be noted here that the traditional method of cutting into the snake bite wound, cleaning it, and applying a tourniquet is now considered most inappropriate. Treatment should now consist of first washing or flushing excess venom off skin and then applying a firm broad bandage to the entire bitten limb, keeping the patient inactive and seeking immediate medical advice.

BIRDS

Of the approximately seven hundred and twenty five species of birds in Australia about one hundred have been recorded in the rainforests of the Wet Tropics. Most of these birds are restricted to, or have the bulk of their distribution in, rainforest. Twelve species are endemic, or peculiar, to the rainforests of the Wet Tropics. Most endemics dwell in upland forests and these include Bower's Shrike-thrush, Australian Fernwren, Atherton Scrubwren, Mountain Thornbill, Bridled Honeyeater, Golden Bowerbird and Tooth-billed Bowerbird. The other endemics, the Lesser Sooty Owl, Chowchilla, Pied Monarch, Macleay's Honeyeater and Victoria's Riflebird, occur at all altitudes.

Some birds, such as the Grey-headed Robin and the much rarer Blue-faced Finch, occur in our wet tropical rainforests and also in New Guinea. Other species such as the Southern Cassowary, Red-necked Crake, Papuan Frogmouth and Spotted Catbird occur in the Wet Tropics, on Cape York Peninsula and in New Guinea. The Metallic Starling and Buff-breasted Paradise-kingfisher migrate between Australia and New Guinea seasonally, coming south to breed in summer. Many other widespread Australian birds, such as the Eastern Whipbird, Pale-yellow Robin and Satin Bowerbird, have populations, treated as distinct subspecies, endemic to the Wet Tropics. Further details are given below under species accounts.

Southern Cassowary
Casuarius casuarius

This huge flightless bird, like the New Zealand Kiwis, Ostriches of Africa, Rheas of South America and our familiar Emu, is a remnant of the avian past known as a ratite.

Heavy dense plumage, horny-looking casque atop the skull, and three to five odd large wire-like feather quills that extend from the vestigial wings, are believed to provide protection for the bird in its rainforest environment. As it runs quickly through the forest the head is lowered, casque held upright, and plumage and wing quills held out to brush aside impeding foliage. Other than its dense blue-black feathering, the adult cassowary sports bright hues of red and blue bare skin about the head and neck and bare pendulose red neck wattles, doubtless as conspicuous social signals to others of its kind. Immature birds have brown feathering, lack a casque, and have paler, pinkish or yellowish, wattles. Cassowary legs are large and powerful, the inner pair of huge toes are tipped with dagger-like nails, and birds may weigh up to fifty five kilograms.

Female cassowaries, which are larger than males, are promiscuous and may lay eggs in the egg scrapes (not a nest really) of several males, only to leave each male with the family duties of incubating the huge one to five blue-green eggs (**right**) and caring for the newly-hatched brown and cream striped chicks (**back cover**).

The Southern Cassowary inhabits rainforests of the Wet Tropics, Cape York Peninsula and New Guinea. New Guinea is home to two other cassowary species, the larger lowland Northern, or Single-wattled, Cassowary and the Dwarf Cassowary of the highlands.

Grey Goshawk
Accipiter novaehollandiae

The Grey Goshawk is by no means limited to the Wet Tropics or to tropical rainforests; being found throughout northern, eastern and south-eastern Australia in forests and woodlands of all kinds. It is true to say, however, that this bird is the true avian diurnal predator of the wet tropical rainforests. Its presence is made known, as soon as it takes flight, by the alarm calls and sudden dashes to cover of numerous small forest birds. All but the largest of bird species are potential prey to the Grey Goshawk. We once came upon an individual that had just killed and plucked a Spotted Catbird (see page 57), itself no mean killer of small birds.

Grey Goshawks occur in two distinct plumage forms – pure white or grey. The bird illustrated (**left**) is of the grey form.

Australian Brush-turkey
Alectura lathami

The Brush-turkey (**left below**)) is found from Cape York Peninsula southwards to eastern Queensland and north-east New South Wales to Sydney. This bird and the Orange-footed Scrubfowl (see page 40) and Malleefowl of arid southern Australia constitute the three Australian representatives of the family Megapodidae or mound-builders. The family name alludes to the large feet of these birds, used to both build nest mounds and to forage for food. Brush-turkeys live in a wide range of habitats, including rainforests, the landward edge of mangroves, dense vine thickets and even more open and barren areas. In the Wet Tropics they are common in rainforests and are invariably encountered around regularly used picnic tables and camping grounds where they take advantage of human visitors. These birds feed rather like domestic fowls, scraping away leaf litter with their large feet and pecking at exposed foods. They are omnivorous and feed upon seeds, fruits, small invertebrates and carrion.

Males of these large terrestrial birds accumulate vast mounds of leaf litter and earth by scratching with their large feet. These mounds are in fact incubator nests, in which females will lay eggs. The male will subsequently care for them, by maintaining the temperature and humidity within the mound at the optimum for egg incubation. This is done by the industrious bird adding or subtracting mound material to compensate for changes in climate. Brush-turkey mounds may be some four metres in diameter and one to two metres high. A quick look at the surrounding forest floor will tell the observer if the mound is actively in use, for if it is the ground will be scraped quite clean of debris. The tail of the Brush-turkey is remarkable in being held on a vertical axis, which it fans and closes during social encounters, possibly to indicate dominance or submissiveness. This alignment of the tail is also advantageous in a bird that constantly throws ground debris behind it.

The population of birds in this area have bright yellow wattle skin, but in the northern population on Cape York Peninsula this skin is a delicate purple-mauve.

Orange-footed Scrubfowl
Megapodius reinwardt

The Orange-footed Scrubfowl (**right**) is confined strictly to the tropics in Australia. It is widespread in New Guinea, Indonesia and the South Pacific islands. The Scrubfowl is very vocal indeed, producing weird and wonderful extremely loud crows, cries and screams, often throughout the night. Nest mounds (see Australian Brush-turkey text) vary considerably in size. Some mounds have been found as large as twelve metres in diameter and five metres high, but most are much smaller.

Red-necked Crake
Rallina tricolor

This attractive rail (**right below**) has a distinctive brilliant chestnut head, neck and breast in the adult plumage. Immature birds lack the rich reddish plumage and are predominantly greyish. Despite the bright adult plumage, birds may prove very difficult to see in the dense tropical rainforest habitat. The distinctive Red-necked Crake call may be heard, however, as it produces a very loud repeated series of sharp *keck* notes which diminish in power and clarity; usually given at dawn and dusk or during very overcast dark weather. Although this rail is rare and restricted in its range to the Wet Tropics and Cape York Peninsula within Australia it is widespread through New Guinea, the Moluccas and the Bismarck Archipelago.

Superb Fruit-dove
Ptilinopus superbus

Seen here is a male Superb, or Purple-crowned, Fruit-dove sitting tightly on his nest and young one (**opposite above**). The photograph gives the impression that this colourful bird would be conspicuous anywhere, even in its lush green rainforest home, but this is far from the case. It is in fact only the males that sport the purple crown and other gaudy colours. The females are generally green save a deep purple rear crown patch. The birds deep repeated 'whoop' call note is often heard in lowland and highland rainforest, but birds are seldom seen until they are flushed into their whirring-winged flight.

Wompoo Fruit-dove
Ptilinopus magnificus

The Wompoo Fruit-dove is one of the most splendid of all the lovely fruit doves, and its loud 'wampoo' or 'wollack-a-woo' calls are a familair sound in the canopy of our tropical rainforests. The photograph (**opposite below**) shows this magnificent fruit-dove feeding in the Native Nutmeg tree. When the nutmeg fruits are ripe they split open to expose the bright red edible aril which encloses the seed. It is also a favourite food of Torresian Imperial, or Nutmeg, Pigeons. The Rose-crowned Fruit-dove, Topknot Pigeon, White-headed Pigeon, Emerald Pigeon and Brown Cuckoo-dove also occur in the rainforests of the Wet Tropics.

41

Australian King Parrot
Alisterus scapularis

The first sighting of this magnificent bird in the wild is always a moment of intense pleasure to all who experience it. The species is widespread along the eastern and south-eastern zone of Australia. Birds encountered in the wet tropical rainforests are part of a population, given separate subspecies status, that is confined to the Wet Tropics. A smaller population, apparently isolated, occurs in the Eungella Range, near Mackay. The loud characteristic *crassak-crassak* flight call often first attracts the observer to the presence of a pair, or flock, of king parrots. Birds maintain contact with one another with high-pitched piping notes. Foods include fruits, nuts, seeds, blossom, nectar and buds. Seen here (**right**) is a male watching his mate feeding upon fallen rainforest fruits.

Double-eyed Fig-parrot
Psittaculirostris diophthalma

This exquisite little bird is Australia's smallest parrot. It has three distinct forms on the east coast of Australia, two in tropical north-eastern Australia and one further south which is now extremely rare. The northern population, which the photograph depicts (**right below**), occurs in the vine forests on Cape York Peninsula. The central population is found in the lowland and upland rainforests of the Wet Tropics. In this latter population males have less red than the illustrated northern bird, and females have a red patch on the forehead and a buff, as opposed to a yellow, cheek area. These diminutive parrots are seed-eaters and feed mostly on figs.

Crimson Rosella
Platycercus elegans

This familiar and popular bright parrot is widespread throughout much of south-eastern Queensland, New South Wales, Victoria and eastern South Australia. A population of smaller and darker-red birds (**opposite**), given separate subspecies status, is isolated and restricted to the tropical upland forests from Eungella northward almost to Cooktown. Food consists predominantly of seeds but fruits, berries, buds, shoots, blossom and some insects are taken. This bird is often seen eating the seeds of the sarsaparilla tree which vigorously colonizes the edges of roads and clearings in rainforest.

Other parrots encountered within, but are far more widespread than, the rainforests of the Wet Tropics include the Red-tailed Black and Sulphur-crested Cockatoos and the Rainbow and Scaly-breasted Lorikeets. The extremely noisy and colourful lorikeets are often seen in wet tropical forests taking nectar from flowers such as those of umbrella or euodia trees (**page 20 & 21**). As an adaptation to this diet lorikeets have a tongue that has a 'brush' at its tip to enable them to lap up flower nectar. They also eat some seeds, as well as blossom, fruits and insects.

Lesser Sooty Owl
Tyto multipunctata

All sooty owls in Australia were long considered to constitute one species, the Sooty Owl, which occurred in two distinct populations; larger and darker birds living along the south-eastern coastal zone from Melbourne up to the Brisbane area, and smaller paler birds in the Wet Tropics area. Recently some ornithologists have given species status to the isolated northern wet forest and rainforest-dwelling population and called it the Lesser Sooty Owl (**right**).

The Lesser Sooty Owl is a most voracious nocturnal predator and includes in its diet insects, birds, rodents and possums. The characteristic 'falling bomb' call is a loud descending whistling note that may be heard by folk spending the night in or close to rainforests of the Wet Tropics.

Papuan Frogmouth
Podargus papuensis

This magnificent large frogmouth is confined to tropical rainforests and other dense tropical vegetation of the Wet Tropics and Cape York Peninsula, as well as occurring in New Guinea and islands. In place of the striking yellow iris of the commoner and more familiar Tawny Frogmouth, a close relative, this species has a deep blood-red eye (**right below**).

Frogmouths are closely related to owls but are members of a different family of birds and as such are quite distinct in many respects. Their feet are quite small and are weak, being adapted for perching only, and are no use for capturing prey, unlike the powerful talons of owls. As their name implies, frogmouths have huge mouths used to snap up large insects, frogs, lizards, mice and other small animals from the ground and vegetation.

Buff-breasted Paradise-kingfisher
Tanysiptera sylvia

This truly handsome kingfisher has recently been given its unwieldy common name to replace the better known name of White-tailed Kingfisher. It migrates south from New Guinea to breed in lowland rainforests of Cape York Peninsula and the Wet Tropics, moving southward to its breeding grounds. The birds arrive in early November and noisily establish small territories which must contain the bulbous termite mounds, usually on the ground, into which they will excavate a tunnel and nest chamber. The females, which have shorter central tail feathers, incubate the eggs and are then assisted by the male (**opposite**) in feeding one to three noisy young on insects, spiders, frogs and lizards.

Young leave the nest in January or February quite capable of adequate flight. Once their offspring are independent of them the adult birds return to New Guinea, leaving the young birds to find their own way northward several weeks later.

Azure Kingfisher
Ceyx azurea

Although widespread in northern and eastern Australia, this beautiful kingfisher (**opposite above**) is frequently seen in the Wet Tropics along rainforested creeks that support foods and have suitable banks for nesting. Using its bill as a digging tool it excavates a long tunnel into the bank, and enlarges the terminal end of it into a nest chamber where four to seven white eggs are laid. The Azure and the Little Kingfisher (see below) are the only two, of ten, kingfishers in Australia, that typically feed by diving into water for their prey.

Little Kingfisher
Ceyx pusilla

The Litte Kingfisher is the smallest of the ten species of kingfishers breeding in Australia. It occurs in tropical Australia, New Guinea and surrounding islands. It frequents rainforested creeks and, like the Azure Kingfisher, typically dives into water for its prey. This brilliantly plumaged little bird (**opposite below**) is most commonly encountered alone, unless a breeding pair is seen. The nest is a tunnel into a mud bank or termite mound which terminates in a small chamber where five to six white eggs are laid.

Laughing Kookaburra
Dacelo novaeguineae

This bird requires no introduction to Australians, or to many overseas visitors. Whilst it is Australia's best known kingfisher, it is most unlike the kingfishers familiar to Europeans and Americans. More typical kingfishers make their living by hunting aquatic prey; plunging into lakes, ponds or streams to catch fish, crustaceans and other animals. Kookaburras, however, are terrestrial giant kingfishers that hunt small mammals and birds, snakes, lizards and numerous insects and other arthropods on dry land. Whilst the Kookaburra's immediate relative, the Blue-winged Kookaburra, is Australia's truly tropical kookaburra it is the more familiar and widespread Laughing Kookaburra (**left above**) that sometimes inhabits rainforests within the Wet Tropics.

Noisy Pitta
Pitta versicolor

The brightly coloured Noisy Pitta (**left**) makes its presence obvious in summer by a loud and clearly whistled 'walk-to-work' call. The typical habitat is rainforest, but adjacent woodlands and mangroves are also frequented. Nesting takes place on the ground, in low vegetation or on tree buttresses, the nest being a domed structure with a side entrance; often with a ramp of sticks, mosses and leaves as a 'doorstep'. Some Noisy Pittas migrate to New Guinea each year, some move from highland breeding areas to lowland and offshore-island wintering grounds, and others simply remain resident all year round.

Pale-yellow Robin
Tregellasia capito

This appealing little robin occurs in two quite isolated populations on the east Australian coast. Birds of the northern population (**right**) are found only within the Wet Tropics where they associate primarily with rainforest and denser vegetation on water courses. Birds typically use vertical saplings while surveying the ground for prey animal movement. The Pale-yellow Robin appears to associate closely with Lawyer Cane (see page 16) when nesting, and uses the viciously-spiked main stems of these plants to nest on, thereby attaining some defence from nest predators.

Robins belong to a group of birds called the flycatchers, which also includes the thrushes, of the family Muscicapidae. Several members of this family occur in rainforests of the Wet Tropics, including the Bassian Thrush, Golden Whistler, Grey Whistler, Bower's Shrike-thrush, Little Shrike-thrush, Yellow-breasted Boatbill, Pied Monarch, Black-faced Monarch, Spectacled Monarch, Rufous Fantail and Grey Fantail.

Grey-headed Robin
Poecilodryas albispecularis

Many Australian robins (not strictly speaking true robins but more correctly members of the flycatcher group) are brightly coloured in strong reds, pinks and yellows, but the Grey-headed Robin is as beautiful and striking in a more subtle range of tortoiseshell hues (**opposite**). This large robin occurs in mid and upland rainforests of the Wet Tropics, above 200 metres altitude, and also in New Guinea. Although often hard to see, its monotone single soft-repeated whistle note is very characteristic of the southern forests of the Wet Tropics, but in the forests inland of Cairns and northward it also gives a two note whistle.

Bassian Thrush
Zoothera lunulata

A widespread population of birds previously known as White's or the Scaly Thrush, distributed from the Atherton Tableland down the Australian east coast to Victoria, Tasmania and eastern South Australia, was in 1984 demonstrated to include two different species. The Bassian Thrush occurs in two forms, one in South Australia, Victoria and Tasmania, eastern New South Wales and south-eastern Queensland and another (**right**), in the highland rainforests of Wet Tropics. The other species, now known as the Russet-tailed Thrush, occurs in north-eastern New South Wales and south-eastern central coastal and north-eastern Queensland, where it meets the Bassian Thrush.

The Bassian Thrush is a shy ground-frequenting bird that feeds singly or in pairs on insects, worms, other invertebrates and some fruit. It frequently utters subdued high-pitched whistles, but may at times also produce a song which is reminiscent of the calls of the European Blackbird.

Bower's Shrike-thrush
Colluricincla boweri

Two of Australia's four shrike-thrush species occur in the wet tropical rainforests. Bower's Shrike-thrush is the least known of the four and is confined to the upland regions of rainforests of the Wet Tropics above 400 metres altitude. It is a difficult bird to see notwithstanding its loud, commonly heard, 'chuck' call and varied whistled notes. At the forest edges this bird may be confused with the Little, or Rufous, Shrike-thrush, from which it can be differentiated by its blackish bill, less white throat and much greyer back. It is an active foliage-gleaner taking insects and other invertebrates from leaves and vine tangles, and it commonly tears apart dry dead vegetation.

One result of our studies of some of the birds in wet tropical rainforests is the finding that, contrary to previous opinion, the sexes of Bower's Shrike Thrush are clearly distinguishable. The female (**right**) has a conspicuous eye-ring and an eye-brow of pale rufous feathers which is absent in the male. The shrike-thrushes are very closely related to the whistlers, and can in fact be viewed as being little more than drab whistlers. Like the true whistlers, the shrike-thrushes are very fine songsters.

It is worth noting here that the calls of the Bower's Shrike-thrush are some of the most regularly mimicked by that remarkable mimic the Tooth-billed Bowerbird (see page 58). This ability to mimic other bird calls so well makes bird identification by calls alone difficult in upland wet tropical rainforests during the summer months.

Yellow-breasted Boatbill
Machaerirhynchus flaviventer

The Yellow-breasted Boatbill is truly a bird of the tropics; where it can be seen in rainforests, dense vegetation along creeks and in adjacent woodlands. The Yellow-breasted Boatbill is the most peculiar of our Australian flycatchers, its very broadly flattened beak being a quite unique adaptation, that is apparently for snatching up insects.

The adult male is a strikingly marked bright yellow, black and white bird; the upperparts being mostly jet black marked with white. A conspicuous eyestripe and the underparts are yellow and the throat is white. The female is a much lighter and duller yellow and is olive on the back where he is black. Some breeding females retain the distinctly barred immature ventral plumage, as was the case in the nest we photographed (**right**). Fully adult-plumaged females have pure yellow underparts.

Both sexes of the breeding pair take part in nest building, incubating the clutch of two eggs and provisioning the young. The tiny suspended nest is extremely difficult to find and, as it may be built between four to twenty metres above ground, a lot of skill or luck is required to find one low enough to study and photograph.

Spectacled Monarch
Monarcha trivirgatus

The Spectacled Monarch is not confined to the tropics, occurring southward to Sydney in New South Wales, but it is a bird very typical of the rainforests of the Wet Tropics. This active bird can be seen singly or in pairs in the middle and lower levels of the rainforest where it flutters and hops through the foliage in search of insects. Its noisy chattering calls are conspicuous and characteristic.

The sexes of this monarch are generally similar in appearance, although females are somewhat duller in their colours than males. The nest is typically constructed in the fork of a small sapling, or between vine stems, and two young are usually raised (**left**). The slight differences between the sexes in the adult plumages of the Spectacled Monarch have not yet enabled observers to determine the division of labour between the sexes at the nest.

This is one of eleven Australian birds known collectively as monarch flycatchers; others to occur in this region being the, widespread, Black-faced Monarch and the Pied Monarch which is endemic to the Wet Tropics region.

Pied Monarch
Arses kaupi

The Pied Monarch is truly endemic to the rainforests of the Wet Tropics. It is very similar to its close relative the Frilled Monarch of Cape York Peninsula. The sexes in both the Pied and the Frilled Monarch differ in the same way, the chin of males being black whereas it is white in the females. The illustrated individual (**left**) is an immature female. Adult birds have a blue bill. The bare orbital skin is blue in both adult sexes of both species, giving these birds a particularly attractive look. Both species are small black and white birds with unusual erectile nape frills.

The nests of the Pied and Frilled Monarchs are distinctly different to those of other Australian monarch flycatchers. They consist of delicate and beautiful frail cup-shaped baskets of fine dry twiglets, rootlets and vine tendrils loosely woven and bound together with spider webs and decorated on the outside with pieces of lichen. These structures are slung, hammock-like, between vertical hanging vine stems. Two eggs form the clutch which may be found mostly between September and January. Both the Frilled and Pied Monarchs are active birds, ceaselessly foraging for insect prey on tree trunks and larger boughs, clinging to the bark and clambering and fluttering upwards and downwards.

Chowchilla
Orthonyx spaldingii

One of only two species of logrunner, the Chowchilla or Northern Logrunner is a very different bird from its more widespread and smaller relative of eastern New South Wales and extreme south-eastern Queensland. The Chowchilla lives in both highland and lowland rainforests of the Wet Tropics where its conspicuous and loud early morning calls dominate the dawn chorus.

Chowchillas are more often heard than seen as their plumage and cryptic behaviour effectively camouflages them against their dim forest floor backdrop. By following the direction of their calls and then, when closer, looking for moving leaf litter a flock of chowchillas can be watched. These birds, in which the female has a rufous breast (**right**) and the male has it white, are constantly active on the forest floor. They run and hop about in small flocks of about four to six birds and defend a territory by calling along its perimeter. They feed by grasping leaf litter in one foot and throwing it away from them to one side while searching intently for animals which are then snatched up in the bill. In order to do this comfortably, without falling off the single leg left supporting them, they have a remarkably modified tail which acts as a prop, rather like people use a shooting stick. The central shafts of the tail feathers have been thickened into very strong spines, which give the bird the alternative name of Spalding's Spinetail. Leaning back and down onto this useful support the bird obtains the considerable leverage required to tear and pull at the forest floor. A frantically feeding bird is amusing to watch as it continuously hurls debris about itself, appearing to almost drop out of sight beneath the litter into holes it digs for itself.

Eastern Whipbird
Psophodes olivaceus

Bird lovers of central eastern and south-eastern Australia need no introduction to this bird (**right**), for its famous sharp whip-crack-like call is familiar to all that live within its range. The bulk of this bird's distribution is from Melbourne east and northward to the Eungella Range near Mackay in Queensland. A population also exists, and is acknowledged to form a distinct subspecies, in the Wet Tropics area where it lives primarily at higher altitudes in rainforest.

Whilst the Eastern Whipbird is well known, and much loved for its call, it is a shy retiring species that can be difficult to see and observe. Birds of the Wet Tropics populations have an additional 'chip-chop chip-chop' call that initially confuses southern birdwatchers. Eastern Whipbirds search for their diet of various arthropods primarily close to and on the forest floor, usually in pairs. The loud vocalisations are doubtless an effective means of maintaining contact in the dense forest understorey. Occasionally whipbirds may be seen foraging higher in the rainforest strata, amongst fallen debris accumulated atop large epiphytic plants, such as bird's nest, elkhorn or staghorn ferns (see page 12).

Australian Fernwren
Crateroscelis gutturalis

This diminutive bird (**left**) is strictly confined to the upland rainforest areas of the Wet Tropics, above about 600 metres above sea level. Whilst it is quite vocal, producing very drawn-out, high-pitched whistles and scolding notes, it is rather retiring and difficult to see unless by a lone, still, and patient observer. It hops actively over the forest floor leaf litter, turning over individual leaves and small amounts of debris with its fine tweezer-like bill in search of small arthropods. A remarkable aspect of this bird's breeding biology is its relatively huge and solid domed nest of rootlets and mosses which is attached to a tree trunk, creek bank or small cave wall. Two white eggs are laid, between August and February, and the nestlings are provisioned by both parents. The female is a slightly duller version of the male.

The Fernwren belongs to the family Acanthizidae. Other members of this family to be seen in rainforests of the Wet Tropics include the Mountain Thornbill (see page 55), Brown Gerygone, Large-billed Gerygone, Fairy Gerygone and three species of scrubwrens (see below).

Large-billed Scrubwren
Sericornis magnirostris

Three scrubwren species commonly occur in the area of rainforest within the Wet Tropics; the Large-billed Scrubwren, the Atherton Scrubwren and the Yellow-throated Scrubwren. An additional species, the White-browed Scrubwren, may be seen at the rainforest edge. The Large-billed Scrubwren occurs down much of the eastern coastal zone of Australia, where it is found in three isolated populations. The northernmost of these populations is confined to the Wet Tropics area and is recognised as a separate subspecies. The Large-billed Scrubwren forages in understorey vegetation in small flocks. It is seen here (**left**) clinging to its feather-lined domed nest about to feed its young.

The Atherton Scrubwren, as its name implies, is peculiar to the wet tropical rainforest from the Thornton Peak and Mount Windsor Tableland, southward to Tully Falls, where it co-exists with the northern population of the Large-billed Scrubwren. The Atherton Scrubwren was long overlooked as a good species because it looked almost identical to the Large-billed Scrubwren. The Atherton Scrubwren lives in rainforest, mostly above 600 metres altitude. It is far more terrestrial than the Large-billed Scrubwren, and forages in pairs or in small parties for its small arthropod food found mostly on leaf litter and lower vegetation. Unlike the Large-billed Scrubwren, the Atherton Scrubwren has a faint pale eyestripe above the eye, is slightly longer in the leg, and has a darker face.

The Yellow-throated is perhaps the most vocal and easily noticed of scrubwrens. It is a terrestrial species, specializing in feeding upon the forest floor litter. It has an upland-dwelling population in the Wet Tropics and a more extensively distributed population along the New South Wales coastal zone, to just north of Brisbane in Queensland.

54

Mountain Thornbill
Acanthiza katherina

Of the twelve thornbills in Australia the Mountain Thornbill is the only one confined to the tropics, where it is endemic to the rainforested highlands of the Wet Tropics above 450 metres altitude. Its lovely whitish eyes (**opposite above**) make it easy to identify. It is a foliage foraging bird, actively searching in small flocks for insects amongst the outer leaves of tree canopies. The birds at times produce sweet and melodious clear songs. The nest is a lovely compact dome of fine grasses and fibres decorated outside with mosses and lichens.

Macleay's Honeyeater
Xanthotis macleayana

This is another bird that is restricted to the Wet Tropics. It inhabits rainforested ranges and rainforest, woodland and riverine vegetation of the lowlands. Macleay's Honeyeater (**opposite below**) is not usually an easy bird to see well in rainforest because it remains higher than many other honeyeaters, where it feeds upon flower nectar. Many species of honeyeaters, in particular the Eastern Spinebill, play an important role in the pollination of rainforest flowers.

Yellow-spotted Honeyeater
Meliphaga notata

This (**left above**) is an exclusively tropical honeyeater that occurs together with two very closely related and similar species; the Graceful Honeyeater, of identical distribution, and the far more widespread Lewin's Honeyeater. All three are very similar in appearance and are often difficult to identify unless calls are heard or more than one species can be seen together for direct comparison. The Graceful and the Yellow-spotted Honeyeaters are similar in their appearance but the former is slightly smaller, is paler below, and has a proportionately longer and slimmer bill than the latter. The Lewin's Honeyeater tends to be more of an upland species in the Wet Tropics, is a larger bird, has a larger yellow ear mark spot and a grey, not a brown, eye.

Bridled Honeyeater
Lichenostomus frenatus

The Bridled Honeyeater (**left**) is primarily a bird of tropical highland rainforests, although it can be seen in some lowland locations such as at Cape Tribulation. It also occurs in wet forests along watercourses, swamp woodlands, and in drier forests adjacent to rainforests. Birds can sometimes be seen pressing home vigorous attacks upon another, and birds gripping each other and tumbling down onto the forest floor are not infrequently observed during the breeding season. This bird is particularly fond of feeding from flowering Climbing Pandanus (see page 16) and the Umbrella Tree (see page 20).

Metallic Starling
Aplonis metallica

Also called the Shining Starling, this **(right)** is the only member of the large old world starling family native to Australia (and New Guinea and islands). It migrates from New Guinea to tropical north-eastern Queensland each year (July to September) to breed; returning north between February and April. It builds a large hanging pear-shaped nest of twigs and tendrils suspended from a tree branch with a side entrance partly obscured by a funnel or spout. This is unlike the majority of starlings, which nest in holes. It is gregarious when breeding, nesting in colonies of up to hundreds of pairs.

Flocks of birds can often be heard chattering away in vine forests, mangroves and woodlands in search of fruits. This lovely starling is another bird important to the dispersal of rainforest tree and vine seeds. An examination of the forest floor beneath a nesting colony will result in the finding of a most impressive carpet, often inches deep, of plant seeds that birds have voided. Many of the seeds may germinate and grow to seedlings beneath the nest tree. Countless other seeds are of course dropped by the birds all over the wet tropical rainforests, where they too may succeed in growing into seedlings and subsequently into mature, fruiting, plants.

Yellow Oriole
Oriolus flavocinctus

All three members of the oriole family found in Australia occur within the Wet Tropics but only the Yellow Oriole and the Figbird are encountered in rainforests. The Olive-backed Oriole may in fact sometimes be found at the edge of rainforest, but is far more typically a bird of eucalypt forests and woodlands throughout eastern and tropical Australia. The Olive-backed Oriole can be readily distinguished from the Yellow Oriole by the former's black-streaked white underparts and grey wings and tail.

The Yellow Oriole **(right)**, an exclusively tropical species within Australia, is characteristic of the rainforests of the Wet Tropics but far more so of the lowlands than of the uplands. It also lives in New Guinea. Its distinctive powerful loud bubbling call of three to four varied notes are characteristic where pairs are in residence. It feeds almost exclusively on tropical fruits, but doubtless feeds young birds some insect foods. The nest is a deep substantial cup of tree bark, grass and leaves, bound with cob-webs and suspended by its rim from a horizontal fork of the outer branches of trees, two to twenty metres above ground. Two or three cream or pale brown coloured eggs, blotched and spotted with dark pigment, are laid. Little else is known about the breeding biology of this lovely bird.

Victoria's Riflebird
Ptiloris victoriae

Named after the British Queen, Victoria's Riflebird is one of the fabulous birds of paradise for which New Guinea is particularly well known. Australia is, however, home to four of the forty two birds of paradise; two of them being other kinds of riflebirds and the fourth the Trumpet Manucode that occurs in vine forests of Cape York Peninsula. The Magnificent Riflebird is a widespread New Guinea species that also occurs on Cape York Peninsula. The Paradise Riflebird occurs on ranges between approximately Rockhampton in Queensland southward to just north of Sydney, New South Wales. Victoria's Riflebird is, however, entirely endemic to the rainforests of the Wet Tropics.

Riflebirds are typical birds of paradise. The ornate male (**left**) is a promiscuous bird that calls from and displays on a number of courtship perches within his territory. The penetrating loud calls of a male riflebird advertise his presence to potential mates, and to rival males, and when a female arrives near his display branches he goes into intense display to impress her. Throwing his peculiarly rounded wings up either side of the upstretched head and neck the bird erects much of his lovely velvet and metallic plumage and sways slightly from side to side and bobs up and down while rapidly flicking his head, first to one wing edge and then to the other. Occasionally the long bill is opened to reveal the brilliant yellow mouth interior which is a startling display feature within the darkness of the forest. Females visit males, compare them, and select the finest to mate with. Females alone build the nest and care for the eggs and young.

Riflebirds have very powerful legs and claws which they use to clamber over tree trunks and large boughs. They can often be seen probing beneath tree bark or into rotting wood for insects and insect larvae which constitute much of their diet. They also eat fruit.

Spotted Catbird
Ailuroedus melanotis

There are nineteen species of bowerbirds, of which ten are found in Australia and eleven in New Guinea, two species occurring in both places. Four species occur in the rainforests of the Wet Tropics, all of which are illustrated here (see also page 58).

There are two species of catbirds in Australia. The Spotted Catbird (**left**) occurs in the rainforests of the Wet Tropics and on Cape York Peninsula, and is also found in New Guinea. The closely related Green Catbird, larger and more uniformly green, occurs in the rainforests of the south-eastern corner of Queensland and eastern New South Wales. The reproductive behaviour of catbirds is atypical of bowerbirds inasmuch as a male and a female look identical, form a pair-bond for one to several breeding seasons and defend a territory in which they share the duties of raising the young. Catbirds are named for their cat-like wailing calls. They predominantly eat fruit but parents feed their young a good deal of worms, insects and nestlings of smaller birds.

Tooth-billed Bowerbird
Scenopoeetes dentirostris

Bowerbirds are known world-wide for the remarkable behavioural developments of the males in most species. The bower is constructed to impress potential mates, and perhaps also to deter rival males. Males are promiscuous and spend the breeding season calling and displaying at their bowers in an attempt to mate with many females. Females will then nest build, incubate their one or two eggs, and raise their young entirely alone.

The Tooth-billed Bowerbird is found in upland rainforests of the Wet Tropics, usually higher than 600 metres altitude. The adult male tooth-bill clears a patch of rainforest floor, several square metres in area, of all leaf litter and debris. He then decorates this conspicuously contrasting area with leaves placed paler underside uppermost to produce maximum effect. This is the male's 'court' at which he loudly sings (**right**), typically mimicking the calls of numerous other rainforest bird species, in order to attract females. Visiting females must be suitably impressed by his court, decorations, vocalizations and displays, if they are to mate with him.

Satin Bowerbird
Ptilonorhynchus violaceus

Best known of all bowerbirds is the Satin Bowerbird because of its extensive distribution down the eastern and south-eastern coast of Australia. A population of smaller birds of this species, recognised as a distinct subspecies, occurs in the upland forests of the Wet Tropics. The male Satin Bowerbird builds an 'avenue' bower of two parallel walls of sticks, which he decorates with blue and green objects such as bird feathers, fruit, flowers and numerous man-made objects (**right**). This preference for one or two colours as bower decoration is typical of most bowerbirds. He also 'paints' the bower walls by applying pigmented fruit pulp or other vegetable matter mixed with saliva to inner bower sticks.

Golden Bowerbird
Prionodura newtoniana

The Golden Bowerbird has a very restricted range, being confined to the upland rainforests of the Wet Tropics, mostly higher than nine hundred metres above sea level. It is the world's smallest bowerbird, but builds the largest of bowers (**opposite** and upper left front cover). Males probably do not attain their golden adult plumage until after their sixth or seventh year, and until doing so they wear the olive-grey appearance of females. Their bowers usually consist of one or two towers of sticks, up to three metres tall, with a display perch protruding from a single bower tower, or connecting two towers. Where the tower sticks meet the display perch they are more skillfully laid and aligned. It is on these better constructed areas that decorations are placed. Females are dressed in grey and olive-brown to render them far less conspicuous whilst raising one or two young in a small cup nest built into a tree crevice.

MAMMALS

Twenty species of marsupials have been recorded in the rainforests of the Wet Tropics, and nine of them are peculiar to this region. Six of the endemics are confined to upland forests. These include the Atherton Antechinus, Green Ringtail Possum, Lemuroid Ringtail Possum, Daintree River Ringtail Possum, Herbert River Ringtail Possum and Thornton Peak Melomys. The Lumholtz's Tree-kangaroo dwells mostly in upland areas, but Bennett's Tree-kangaroo and the Musky Rat-kangaroo are also found in the lowlands. The Long-tailed Pygmy Possum is restricted to the Wet Tropics in Australia but also occurs in New Guinea, and the Striped Possum occurs in this region, on Cape York Peninsula, and in New Guinea.

Six species of native rats live in the wet tropical rainforests, but only one, the Thornton Peak Melomys, is endemic. Three familiar Australian animals, the Short-beaked Echidna, the Platypus and the Dingo, also occur here. Some nine species of bats are dependent on wet tropical rainforests for foraging and roosting. The rare Tube-nosed Insectivorous Bat is the only bat restricted to the Wet Tropics in Australia, but it also occurs in South-east Asia.

Yellow-footed Antechinus
Antechinus flavipes

The Yellow-footed Antechinus (**right above**) is one of three species to occur in the rainforests of the Wet Tropics, the others being the Brown Antechinus and the Atherton Antechinus. The latter species is restricted to rainforests above 600 metres altitude.

Antechinuses may be glimpsed during the day scampering quickly over leaf litter or climbing trees. Their diet includes beetles, cockroaches, spiders and other arthropods and they will even eat small reptiles, birds and mice. They breed once a year, usually around July and August. Mating can be a violent affair and last for several hours. The male grips the scruff of the female's neck in his jaws and wraps his forelegs tightly around her abdomen. Soon after mating the males die!

Antechinuses belong to a group of carnivorous marsupials called the Dasyurids. Other dasyurids to be seen in these forests include Spotted-tailed Quoll and, interestingly, the White-footed Dunnart. This population of dunnarts is quite isolated from the main population which lives in heath and more open forests in southern Victoria and Tasmania, some four thousand kilometres away!

Long-nosed Bandicoot
Perameles nasuta

The Long-nosed Bandicoot (**right**) is commonly to be seen at night vigorously digging conical holes in the ground with its front feet. It inserts its long nose into the holes to sniff out insects and other invertebrates. During the day it hides up in a shallow leaf-lined nest hole on the ground. Bandicoots belong to a group of marsupials called the perameloids, which also includes the bilbies of arid central Australia.

Coppery Brushtail Possum
Trichosurus vulpecula

An experience in tropical rainforest not to be missed is spotlighting at night for possums. The first thing one usually sees of an animal is two large eyes, that are well adapted for night vision, staring back down at one from the leafy tree tops. Often a possum sits motionless, as if hypnotized by the light, looking directly back at the observer. The greatest diversity of possum species occurs within the rainforests of the Wet Tropics and within this area, such as at Mount Hypipamee (Crater) National Park, keen possum watchers congregate in the early evening to spotlight. The delightful Coppery Brushtail Possum (**left**) is one of the easiest to see as it often gathers on dusk near picnic tables. It is easily recognised by its prominent pointed ears and splendid reddish-brown coppery coat. Although commonly referred to as the Coppery Brushtail it is in fact a variety of the well known Common Brushtail Possum which is widespread in the open eucalypt woodlands of Australia. It is nocturnal and mainly vegetarian and is known to eat leaves of Wild Tobacco which contain a substance toxic to people but obviously not to these possums. It belongs to a group of marsupials called the phalangerids, which also includes the cuscuses of Cape York Peninsula and New Guinea.

Green Ringtail Possum
Pseudocheirus archeri

Four of Australia's six species of ringtail possum, are endemic to the upland rainforests of the Wet Tropics, namely the Herbert River Ringtail, the Daintree River Ringtail, the Lemuroid Ringtail and the Green Ringtail. These ringtails are considered relics of an ancient and much more extensive rainforest fauna that dates back to Gondwanaland (see page 2).

The appealing Green Ringtail Possum (**left**) is the most widespread of the four ringtails, occuring at altitudes above 300metres, from Mount Windsor Tableland to the Paluma Range (see map, page 71). The greenish colouration of this possum is due to an unusual combination of black, white and yellow pigments, and the structure of its hairs. This is quite different from the Tree Sloth of South America whose renowned greenish fur is due to algal growth. The green fur of this ringtail is blotched with various shades of creamy white to yellow, and is broken up with stripes down the back. This provides excellent camouflage for it within its leafy canopy home, particularly during the day when it sleeps curled up in a tight ball on an open branch rather than in a den like most possums do. Its large protruberant eyes are well adapted for nocturnal vision and are easily picked up when spotlighting at night, as they reflect red light from the back of the eye. It is a delight indeed to see a young possum riding piggy-back on its mother's neck or back. The single young ringtail clings so tightly to its mother's back after it has left the pouch that occasional handfuls of fur are pulled out so that her coat becomes progressively tatty as the young grows.

Herbert River Ringtail Possum
Pseudocheirus herbertensis

The Herbert River Ringtail (**right**) lives at an altitude above about 350 metres, from the Lamb Range on the Atherton Tableland south to the Seaview Range (see map, page 71). This possum is typically dark brown, dark grey or black above, and white below; the head is all-black and the distal half of the tail is usually white. During the day these lovely possums rest in hollow trees or amongst clumps of vegetation such as epiphytic ferns, mistletoe and palm crowns. At early evening they emerge from their daytime retreat and commence their nightime feeding forays. Leaves of rainforest trees form the bulk of their diet although they occasionally eat fruits and flowers of trees such as the Bumpy Satinash (see page 15).

The Herbert River Ringtail, like all the ringtails, is a very efficient tree climber. It is able to grip a branch by opposing the first and second toes of its forefoot against the other three. The long, lightly-furred, prehensile tail functions like a fifth limb and greatly assists possum in its arboreal existence. At rest the tail is carried in a tight coil.

Females generally raise two young at a time. At an early age the young is left in a safe place by the mother who returns to it after foraging trips. The young is uniformly pale brown in colour but changes to the adult black and white colour within a year.

Daintree River Ringtail Possum
Pseudocheirus cinereus

This uniformly caramel coloured possum was first collected in 1937 and described as a subspecies of the Herbert River Ringtail in 1945. It was not recorded again until it was photographed by Stan and Kay Breeden in 1967. In 1989 it was described as a distinct species and was appropriately named the Daintree River Ringtail. It occurs above 450 metres altitude around Thornton Peak on the Mount Windsor Tableland and southward to Mount Lewis on the Mount Carbine Tableland. The charming Daintree River Ringtail (**opposite**) varies in overall colour from pale caramel to a darkish grey on the upperside, the underside being paler; and with a distinctive dark vertical stripe on the forehead. It is arboreal, nocturnal, and predominantly vegetarian, and its general habits are similar to those of the Herbert River Ringtail.

All the ringtails belong to a group of marsupials called the petaurids, that also includes the Striped Possum. Although not illustrated here the delightful black and white Striped Possum can also be seen in rainforests of the Wet Tropics, as well as those of Cape York Peninsula and New Guinea. Unlike the ringtails, however, it eats mostly wood-boring grubs and other insects from tree trunks and rotting logs.

Lemuroid Ringtail Possum
Hemibelideus lemuroides

This woolly-looking possum (**right**) is nocturnal, emerging just after dark to forage almost exclusively on leaves. At night it is often heard clambering noisily around the leafy canopy, especially when it leaps from one branch to another. During the day it usually rests in a tree hollow. Unlike the other ringtails, which tend to be solitary except when breeding, Lemuroid Ringtails are quite sociable and have often be seen in feeding aggregations of up to five members.

The Lemuroid Ringtail Possum occurs on the Mount Carbine Tableland above an altitude of 900 metres, and from the Atherton Tableland south to the Cardwell Range above 480 metres. The tail is more bushy and less tapered than in the other ringtail species. The typical colouring of this ringtail is grey above, with a brownish tinge on the shoulders, and paler below. Individuals of the Mount Carbine Tableland population are smaller and browner than those further south, and about twenty to thirty percent of them are fluffy white with a faint tinge of ginger. The first white Lemuroid was recorded as far back as 1915 but, although seen since then, was photographed for the first time in 1987 (**opposite**, and upper right of front cover).

Females usually produces only one young at a time. The youngster spends much time riding on its mother's back after leaving her pouch, and will often remain with its mother until the next young emerges from the pouch.

Long-tailed Pygmy-possum
Cercartetus caudatus

This tiny marsupial, only some ten centimetres long, belongs to the group of marsupials called the Burramyidae and is very difficult indeed to spot in the rainforest. Although restricted to the upland and lowland forests in the Wet Tropics, it also occurs in New Guinea where this photograph (**right**) was taken. It is nocturnal and arboreal and uses its prehensile tail to climb with agility around small branches. It constructs a nest of leaves in a clump of ferns, a hollow stump, or in a tree hollow. During the day it hides away in the safety of the nest, which is sometimes shared by up to five individuals. At night it emerges to forage on small arthroopods such as crickets, beetles, cockroaches, moths and spiders; and also takes flower nectar from plants such as the Bumpy Satinash (see page 15). The Long-tailed Pygmy-possum raises one to three young. A mother will often defend her young by standing over them on her hindlegs whilst extending her forelegs forward threateningly and hissing quietly at the same time.

These tiny possums are so small that they are not always able to maintain their body heat if it gets very cold or if there is a shortage of food. To overcome this problem they are able to enter into a state of torpor; their body temperature drops to almost that of their surroundings and their breathing rate slows down. They can remain in a state of torpor for up to several days.

Musky Rat-kangaroo
Hypsiprymnodon moschatus

It is hard to imagine that this delightful small Rat-kangaroo (**right**) is most closely related to kangaroos and wallabies, or macropods as they are often referred to. It is in fact the smallest and most primitive macropod and probably represents an early stage in the evolution of them from an arboreal possum-like ancestor. Like the possums, and unlike all the other macropods, it has a mobile first toe on the hind foot which enables it to climb along fallen logs and branches. Although its hindfeet are longer than its fore feet, it generally gallops around in a quadrupedal fashion, that is 'on all fours', unlike the more familiar bipedal gait of kangaroos. Its fur is a lovely rich brown intermingled with darker brown hairs.

The Musky Rat-kangaroo occurs in rainforests of the the Wet Tropics at all altitudes, from just south of Cooktown to the Seaview Range (see map, page 71). Unlike most marsupials it is diurnal. It is often seen scurrying over the forest floor in search of fallen friuits, and it uses its forepaws to turn over leaf litter to find small invertebrates.

At night and during the heat of the day it sleeps in a nest constructed of dried leaves and ferns. Nest building is a complicated job. Firstly the rat-kangaroo collects the nest material with the mouth, then transfers it to its forepaws and then places it on the ground in front of its hindfeet. Its dark brown scaly tail is then curled down and forwards towards the hindfeet and the nest material is kicked into it. The tail clasps the bundle of vegetation and the rat-kangaroo carries it off to its nest site – either in the base of a clump of Lawyer Vine or at the base of a tree buttress!

Red-legged Pademelon
Thylogale stigmatica

The Red-legged Pademelon, as its name suggests, has rufous brown fur on its legs, as well as on its cheeks (**right**). The population in the Wet Tropics is one of three to occur in eastern Australia.

This small compact pademelon inhabits rainforest and adjacent woodlands that have a dense understorey for it to hide away in during the day. When sleeping it adopts a very strange posture indeed. It tucks its tail between its hind legs and, sitting on the base of it, leans back against a tree with its head drooping downwards! On dusk it sets off along well defined and well used runways through dense vegetation to suitable feeding grounds where it is active until shortly before dawn. It grazes on berries, fresh fern fronds, orchids, grasses and other plants, and fallen leaves. It uses its forepaws to hold or manipulate food and will travel on all fours when moving slowly around the forest with its tail dragging behind it. When disturbed, however, it leaps off rapidly on its hind legs.

Lumholtz's Tree-kangaroo
Dendrolagus lumholtzi

It is indeed a shock for many visitors to tropical north Queensland to see (if they are very lucky) kangaroos clambering through the high tree tops, but some members of the family have taken to an arboreal existence. Kangaroos originally evolved by descending, in both senses of the word, from tree-climbing ancestors and adapting to a terrestrial way of life. It is a mystery indeed why some of them then returned to the trees, but tree kangaroos are believed to have done so.

Although several species of Tree-kangaroo occur in New Guinea, only two, Lumholtz's and Bennett's Tree-kangaroos, are found in Australia, and both have a very restricted range within the Wet Tropics. Bennett's Tree-kangaroo occurs in lowland and upland forests in the Daintree area, between Mount Hartley and Mount Windsor Tableland (see map, page 71). Lumholtz's Tree-kangaroo (**left**) occurs on the Mount Carbine Tableland south to the Cardwell Range where it is primarily found in the uplands.

Unlike their ground-dwelling counterparts tree-kangaroos have stout, powerful and heavily clawed fore-legs for gripping branches. Their short and broad hindlegs can move independently when climbing; and their long thick tail provides an important counterbalance for them whilst jumping through the canopy in search of suitable leaf and fruit foods. They are primarily nocturnal. During the day they sleep crouched up on a well hidden canopy branch. Males and females are similar in colour but males attain a larger size.

Spectacled Flying-fox
Pteropus conspicillatus

Many people associate Australia with monotreme and marsupial mammals. Bats and rats, which represent about forty percent of our native fauna, are, however, placental mammals. Many bats forage and/or roost in wet tropical rainforests, including nectar-feeding blossom bats, nectar and fruit-eating flying-foxes, and insectivorous foragers such as horseshoe-bats.

One of the most familiar flying-foxes of these rainforests is the Spectacled Flying-fox (**left**). It is easily recognised by the prominent pale straw-coloured fur around its eyes that suggests a pair of spectacles – hence its common name. Daytime is spent in communal 'camps' which may include tens of thousands of individuals. Camps are usually located in the upper canopy of taller trees in rainforest, swamps and mangroves. It is easy to locate a camp as these fruit bats seldom sleep, but spend much time squawking or squabbling amongst themselves, and the din within a camp is quite deafening. It is an incredible sight indeed to watch thousands upon thousands of bats streaming out from their camp on dusk to embark on nightime foraging forays. The Spectacled Flying-fox feeds on nectar and pollen from blossoms and on fruits of forest trees and palms. They also enjoy citrus fruits and mangoes!

Fawn-footed Melomys
Melomys cervinipes

Two of Australia's four species of melomys occur in the rainforests of the Wet Tropics; the Fawn-footed Melomys and the Thornton Peak Melomys. The Fawn-footed Melomys is found from about Cooktown south to northern New South Wales and is by far the most abundant and commonly seen. The Thornton Peak Melomys was discovered as recently as 1973 and, as its names indicates, has a restricted range within the Wet Tropics.

Melomys are about the size of a rat and have soft, fine, fur and slender, smooth, and almost hairless tails. Melomys and the closely related White-tailed Rat are often referred to as mosaic-tailed rats because the scales on their tails interlock neatly, like floor tiles. Their tails are partly prehensile and support them while climbing by being curled around small branches, and their broad hind feet are well adapted for this arboreal existence. All melomys are very agile and adept climbers and are mostly vegetarian, eating mainly leaves, shoots and fruits.

The Fawn-footed Melomys builds a leafy nest in trees. They reproduce during most of the year and a female may bear up to four young. The young have to cling on tightly to their mother's teats when she is disturbed from the nest (**right**), otherwise they would fall to the ground and be left behind.

White-tailed Rat
Uromys caudimaculatus

The handsome White-tailed Rat (**right**) occurs in the Wet Tropics and on Cape York Peninsula in Australia, but also lives in New Guinea. It is about the size of a small cat or rabbit and can weigh up to one kilogram. It is distinguished from other rodents by its long, slender, almost hairless, scaly, white tail which is tipped black. In the past it has been known by several common names including Giant Rat, Giant White-tailed Rat and Giant Naked-tailed Rat. At present it is simply referred to as the White-tailed Rat!

White-tailed Rats are found mostly in tropical rainforest but also frequent more open-forests and woodlands. They are very efficient tree climbers. The rasp-like scales on their tails and very large strongly-clawed hind feet assist them in their arboreal existence. These rats are mainly nocturnal but may also be glimpsed during the day. They eat fruits and seeds of forest trees, as well as insects, amphibians, bird eggs and nestlings. In some areas they have become a serious pest in coconut plantations, as their strong incisors can easily gnaw into young green nuts on the trees. They also have a reputation as camp robbers, and will carry off tins of food in their powerful jaws!

Other native rodents commonly seen in the wet tropical rainforests include the Bush Rat, the Cape York Rat and the seldom seen Prehensile-tailed Rat. The latter species was known to occur in New Guinea but was first discovered in Australia in 1974 when a cat caught one and brought it into the restaurant at Lake Barrine on the Atherton Tableland!

Further Reading

COGGER, H.G. 1992	Reptiles and Amphibians of Australia Fifth edition, Reed, Sydney
COMMON, I.F.B. & WATERHOUSE, D.F. 1981	Butterflies of Australia 2nd edition, Angus & Robertson, Melbourne
FRITH, C. & FRITH, D. 1989	Australian Tropical Birds Frith & Frith, Malanda
FRITH, C.& FRITH, D. 1991	Australian Tropical Reptiles and Frogs Frith & Frith, Malanda
JONES, D.L. 1986	Ornamental Rainforest Plants in Australia Reed, Sydney
LAVARACK, B. & GRAY, B. 1992	Australian Tropical Orchids Frith & Frith, Malanda
PIZZEY, G. 1980	A Field Guide to the Birds of Australia Collins, Sydney
READERS DIGEST SERVICES 1988	Readers Digest Complete Book of Australian Birds 2nd edition, Readers Digest, Sydney
SLATER, P., SLATER, P. & SLATER, R. 1986	The Slater Field Guide to Australian Birds Weldon, Sydney
STRAHAN, R (Editor) 1983	The Australian Museum Complete Book of Australian Mammals Angus & Robertson, Sydney
VALENTINE, P. 1991	Australian Tropical Butterflies Frith & Frith, Malanda

Photographic Credits

(abbreviations following page numbers are : a = above, b = below)

STANLEY BREEDEN:	67a
ANDREW DENNIS:	upper right of front cover, 65
RALPH & DAPHNE KELLER/ A.N.T. Photo Library:	40a
CLIFF & DAWN FRITH:	all other photographs.

Acknowledgements

We thank staff of Queensland National Parks and Wildlife Service for help in various ways, in particular, Peter Johnson, Bill Laverack and Keith McDonald. Grateful thanks to Peter Valentine for permission to reproduce his, modified, butterfly text. Sincere thanks to Andrew Dennis for proof reading the entire text and to John Winter for commenting on the introductory and mammal sections.

For hospitality, valued company, the provision of photographic subjects and help in other ways we thank Robbie and Judy Bredl, Robyn and Rolly Clarke, Harold Cogger, Bill and Wendy Cooper, Sam and Lisa Dibella, Rupert Russell, Jeff and Jo McClure,

Mike McGuire, Graham and Gill Harrington, Andrew Taplin, Margaret and the late Arthur Thorsborne, Peter and Valerie Valentine, John Young, and Anne-Marie Watt.

We particularly thank Stanley Breeden, Andrew Dennis and Ralph and Daffi Keller for contributing their photographs.

Our own photographs were taken with OLYMPUS OM-4 cameras, accessories and Zuiko lenses with OLYMPUS and METZ flash systems. Camera and flash systems supplied by GUNZ (Photographic) Pty. Ltd. of Sydney, with particular thanks to Bob Pattie. Most film used was Kodachrome 64 KR 135.

Typesetting & Finished Artwork by Law Design Pty Ltd

Printed by Inprint Limited, Australia

Index to Plants and Animals

(Page numbers in boldface are those subjects illustrated)
(fc = front cover; bc = back cover)